Vertebrate Inventory of Whitman Mission National Historic Site 2002-2003

Upper Columbia Basin Network

Natural Resource Technical Report NPS/UCBN/NRTR—2010/280

I0426280

Thomas J. Rodhouse
National Park Service, Upper Columbia Basin Network
Central Oregon Community College, 2600 NW College Way – Ponderosa Building
Bend, OR 97701-5998

Al St. John
2132 NW Cascade View Rd.
Bend, OR 97760

Lisa K. Garrett
National Park Service, Upper Columbia Basin Network
University of Idaho, Department of Fish and Wildlife
Moscow, ID 83844-1136

January 2010

U.S. Department of the Interior
National Park Service
Natural Resource Program Center
Fort Collins, Colorado

The National Park Service, Natural Resource Program Center publishes a range of reports that address natural resource topics of interest and applicability to a broad audience in the National Park Service and others in natural resource management, including scientists, conservation and environmental constituencies, and the public.

The Natural Resource Technical Report Series is used to disseminate results of scientific studies in the physical, biological, and social sciences for both the advancement of science and the achievement of the National Park Service mission. The series provides contributors with a forum for displaying comprehensive data that are often deleted from journals because of page limitations.

All manuscripts in the series receive the appropriate level of peer review to ensure that the information is scientifically credible, technically accurate, appropriately written for the intended audience, and designed and published in a professional manner. This report received formal peer review by subject-matter experts who were not directly involved in the collection, analysis, or reporting of the data, and whose background and expertise put them on par technically and scientifically with the authors of the information.

Views, statements, findings, conclusions, recommendations, and data in this report are those of the author(s) and do not necessarily reflect views and policies of the National Park Service, U.S. Department of the Interior. Mention of trade names or commercial products does not constitute endorsement or recommendation for use by the National Park Service.

This report is available from the Upper Columbia Basin Network website (http://www.nature.nps.gov/im/units/UCBN) and the Natural Resource Publications Management website (http://www.nature.nps.gov/publications/NRPM).

Please cite this publication as:

NPS 371/100878, January 2010

Contents

Contents (continued)

Figures

Tables

Appendices

Abstract

The 2002-2003 Whitman Mission National Historic Site vertebrate inventory developed species lists and additional information on birds, mammals, and herpetofauna at the historic site located in southeastern Washington. The University of Idaho Department of Fish and Wildlife Resources conducted the 2002-2003 inventory under a cooperative agreement with the National Park Service Upper Columbia Basin Network. The primary goal of the inventory was to confirm 90% of the species expected to occur in the mission. Additional goals included developing baseline data for monitoring as well as providing the National Park Service and the research community-at-large with new and important information on the biodiversity of the region.

Expected species lists were developed from available historic sources and expert opinion. A set of four criteria was used to determine the likelihood of detection in the park. Inventory fieldwork utilized a variety of methods to achieve the primary objective, including visual encounter surveys and trapping. Species documentation included the collection of voucher photographs, specimens, and field observation records. Inventory fieldwork was conducted on June 16-21, 2002; August 11-12, 2002; April 1, 2003; April 24, 2003; May 21, 2003; and August 9 and 10, 2003. A 2001 birding field visit by the University of Idaho was included in the 2002-2003 results. Birding observations from Mike Denny, Blue Mountain Audubon Society, are also included in the results. The 2002-2003 inventory was productive and brought species confirmation totals to 100% for birds, 90% for mammals, and 67% for amphibians and reptiles. One hundred seventeen birds were expected to occur in or adjacent to the mission and 202 species were confirmed, including all 117 expected species. Thirty species of mammals were expected in the mission during the inventory and twenty-seven were confirmed. Of the 12 expected species of herpetofauna, 8 species were confirmed. A total of 3 amphibians and 5 reptiles were documented on the mission.

Data from the 2002-2003 inventory has been incorporated into the long-term monitoring program that focused on selected "vital-signs". Future monitoring activities will also provide opportunities to add additional species to the inventory list as they are encountered.

Acknowledgements

The 2002-2003 Whitman Mission National Historic Site vertebrate inventory was made possible through an agreement between the National Park Service Upper Columbia Basin Inventory and Monitoring Network and University of Idaho Department of Fish and Wildlife Resources. We would like to extend a special thanks to Dr. Gerry Wright, USGS Idaho Cooperative Wildlife Research Unit, and Roger Trick, Chief of Historic site Resources for Whitman Mission for providing leadership, direction, and enthusiasm for the project. Historic site staff, especially the maintenance crew, provided invaluable information on vertebrate observations. Special thanks go to Mike Denny of the Blue Mountain Audubon Society for providing a wealth of information on birds in and near the historic site. Thanks are also due to Crystal Strobl, who assisted with fieldwork in June 2002.

Introduction

This report summarizes the results of the 2002-2003 inventory of birds, mammals, and herpetofauna, summarizes historic information, and contains brief accounts of each species present or expected to occur in the Whitman Mission National Historic Site (WHMI). Information on species that are possible but unlikely to occur in the mission is also included.

The 2002-2003 vertebrate inventory was conducted at WHMI by the University of Idaho Department of Fish and Wildlife Resources under a cooperative agreement with the National Park Service Upper Columbia Basin Network. The inventory is part of a nationwide inventory and monitoring (I & M) program funded by the Natural Resource Challenge. In 2000, the Upper Columbia Basin Network, which includes WHMI, began implementing the inventory phase of the I & M program in several of the network parks and monuments. Historic information available on the plant and animal populations within the network were assembled and an estimate was made of the percent of species expected to occur in each park. Whitman Mission was among the majority of network parks that had a low percentage (below 50%) of confirmed species of vertebrates and was in need of a concerted effort to meet the I & M goals.

The primary goal of the inventory phase of the I & M program was to document the presence of 90% of the plant and animal species expected to occur within the historic site boundary or within a distance to the boundary that is relevant to the biology of the organism and to site management. Secondary goals of the inventory included providing baseline information that would help guide the development of the I & M program's vital-signs monitoring strategy. Tertiary goals included providing both the NPS and the research community–at-large new information on the distribution, habitat association, and population status of the nation's biological resources. Ultimately, the I & M program is designed to help the NPS take a leading role in the preservation of the nation's biodiversity. Completing basic biological inventories is a crucial first step in achieving that goal.

Study Area

Whitman Mission National Historic Site is located in the Walla Walla River Valley in southeastern Washington. This small historic site is located 7 miles west of the city of Walla Walla, WA. The historic site commemorates the Whitman Mission that was established along the Oregon Trail in 1836 among the Cayuse Indians and ended in the infamous massacre that eventually led to the establishment of the Oregon Territory. The historic site was established in 1940 and today consists of 98 acres. Ownership patterns adjacent to the historic site consist of a mosaic of private agricultural lands that are influential to the biological diversity of the mission. Wheat, wine, and vegetables have been intensively cultivated in the area for over a century. Figure 1 shows a map of the historic site.

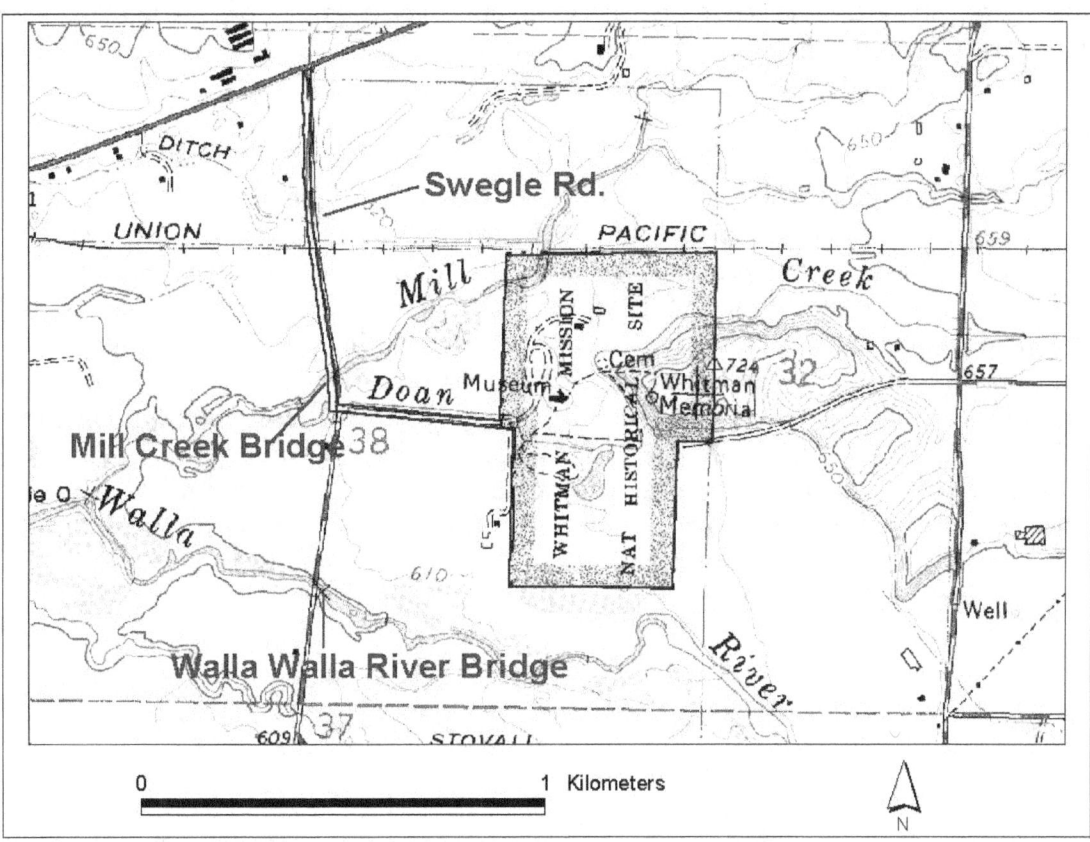

Figure 1. Boundary map of Whitman Mission National Historic Site. The boundary of Whitman Mission formally includes the section of Swegle Road north of the Mill Creek Bridge as well as the entrance road.

Whitman Mission is located between the Walla Walla River and Mill Creek, a tributary of the Walla Walla River. The Walla Walla River flows into the Columbia River approximately 20 miles to the west of the historic site. Elevation of the mission ranges from 720 ft at the top of the memorial hill to 620 ft along the Walla Walla River at the southern boundary of the historic site. The climate in the region is semi-arid, with cool and dry winters and hot and dry summers. Rainfall patterns are variable in the region but most rainfall is recorded in the late fall and winter. Thirty-year mean annual precipitation available from a weather station in Walla Walla is 20 inches (Western Regional Climate Center 2003). Snowfall represents a small proportion of the winter precipitation but snow pack is ephemeral and rarely lasts more than a few days. Thirty-year January and July mean temperatures from Walla Walla are 34 and 75 degrees Fahrenheit, respectively (Western Regional Climate Service 2003). Thirty-year mean January and July minimum and maximum temperatures are 28 and 60 degrees Fahrenheit and 40 and 89 degrees Fahrenheit, respectively (Western Regional Climate Center 2003).

The Walla Walla Valley is located along the southern portion of the Palouse Prairie, consisting of rolling hills of glacial loess (Whitman Mission National Historic Site 2003). This region historically was a vast grassland of perennial bunchgrasses (Whitman Mission National Historic Site 2003). The Cayuse name for the location of the mission was "Waiilatpu", which means "the place of the people of the ryegrass", clearly reflecting the significance of native grasses in the historic landscape (Whitman Mission National Historic Site 2003). However, the deep glacial soils are also extremely fertile and the region was cultivated very early in the settlement era. As a result of this long history of agriculture, the native vegetation in Whitman Mission was almost completely lost until the mid 1980's, when extensive restoration began (Whitman Mission National Historic Site 2003).

The contemporary vegetation in the historic site consists of several different types. The most unique is the small stand of restored upland shrub grassland on the memorial hill, dominated by bluebunch wheatgrass (*Agropyron spicatum*) and gray rabbitbrush (*Chrysothamnus nauseosus*). The majority of the historic site consists of floodplain clays that support extensive stands of Great Basin Wild Rye (*Elymus cinerea*), and exotic weeds such as intermediate wheatgrass (*Agropyron intermedium*), canary reed-grass (*Phalaris arundinacea*) and poison hemlock (*Conium maculatum*). Galleries of cottonwoods (*Populus spp.*) and willows (*Salix spp.*) line the Walla Walla River and Mill Creek. Cultivated stands of black locust (*Robinia pseudo-acacia*) and elm (*Ulmus spp.*) trees are interspersed across mown areas planted with turf near the Mill Pond and around the visitor center and parking lot. Doan Creek, a watercourse intensively modified for irrigation, runs through the middle of the mission and supports dense stands of canary reed-grass along its banks.

Methods

The methods utilized in the 2002-2003 inventory generally followed those laid out in the Upper Columbia Basin Network Study Plan (Wright et. al. unpublished) and published literature on inventory methodologies (i.e. Wilson et. al. 1996). Universal Transverse Mercator (UTM) locations given in this report were collected using Garmin 12-channel Etrex hand-held GPS units (Garmin International, Inc, Olathe, KS, USA). Most x and y coordinates (Easting and Northing) are accurate within 10 meters. The North American Datum of 1927 (NAD 27) was used as the horizontal datum for all locations.

Scientific and common names used in this report follow the Integrated Taxonomic Information System (ITIS). The ITIS follows closely the American Ornithological Union's 7th edition checklist of North American Birds and the USGS Biological Resource Division's unpublished and expanded update of the 1987 Checklist of Vertebrates of the United States, the U.S. Territories, and Canada (ITIS 2003).

The mission boundary was used as the primary boundary of the inventory. However, many species that were observed near the mission were included. This flexibility in boundary was necessary because dispersal abilities of many of the species enable them to move on and off the mission. As well, because birds are so mobile, we have included bird observations made along Swegle Road and Highway 12 (see Figure 1).

Visits to Whitman Mission to conduct inventory activities were made on the following dates; July 15, 2001; June 16-21, 2002; August 11-12, 2002; April 1, 2003; April 24, 2003; May 21, 2003; and August 9 and 10, 2003.

Expected Species

A variety of methods and materials were used to determine which species of birds, mammals, and herpetofauna were expected to occur in the mission. Expert opinion was used to critically examine published range maps and distribution literature from a variety of sources, historic park service reports, and observations. Habitat types occurring in and adjacent to the mission were also carefully considered. Range, elevation, habitat, and species detectability were considered and developed into a criteria set that was used to place species into "expected" and "possible but not expected" categories. Detectability was included in the consideration in order to address species that naturally occur in low abundances or are in some other way very difficult to confirm through established survey protocols. As well, the position of the small historic site within a matrix of agricultural land was also considered and some species that met the four basic criteria but are sensitive to fragmented habitat or to dispersal across inhospitable habitat were not considered as "expected".

Published and unpublished sources used to determine the range, habitat, and elevation requirements of birds, mammals, and herpetofauna included the Peterson Field Guide to Western Birds (Peterson 1990), National Audubon Society Sibley Guide to the Birds (Sibley 2000), Land Mammals of Oregon (Verts and Carraway 1998), Ground-Dwelling Squirrels of the Pacific Northwest (Yensen and Sherman 2003), Reptiles of the Northwest (St. John 2002), Amphibians of Oregon, Washington, and British Columbia (Corkran and Thomas 1996), and the Burke Museum of Natural History and Culture (2003) mammals of Washington on-line publication. Mike Denny (Blue Mountain Audubon Society, Walla Walla, Washington) also provided invaluable information on the birds of the mission based on multiple years of birding experience in the area. The 1962 historic site management plan contained a comprehensive list of birds that was used in the development of the expected bird species list. Former Whitman Mission ranger Jack Winchell also provided invaluable information on historic vertebrate sightings.

Sampling Site Selection
A subjective, non-random sampling site selection procedure was adopted for the 2002-2003 inventory. This approach was determined to be the most efficient and effective given the primary objective of the inventory and the limited number of field personnel. Specific habitats and locations were identified and targeted for sampling in order to maximize the opportunities to encounter as many previously undocumented species as possible. Seasonal changes in species presence or detectability were also an issue and required multiple visits to sites in different seasons. In the case of birds, migrants and winter residents comprise a significant proportion of the expected species and we relied heavily on birding results from local birders to determine the presence of those species.

Visual Encounter Surveys
The visual encounter survey was the primary method used to inventory birds and herpetofauna during the 2002-2003 inventory. Visual encounter surveys were conducted by methodically searching target habitats. Cover turning was incorporated into the herpetological survey and dipnets were used in the Mill Pond to search for amphibians. Weather was a significant factor in the herpetological survey, and searches were normally conducted during times and days when temperature, wind, and precipitation were optimal for reptile and amphibian activity. Incidental observations made of all vertebrates in or near the mission during travel and other inventory activities were included under the visual encounter category as well. Incidental observations contributed significantly to the overall success of the inventory and enabled participation from volunteers and NPS staff. Visual encounter data for birds collected by Mike Denny of the Blue Mountain Audubon Society (Walla Walla, Washington) were also an important component of the visual encounter survey. Ancillary information recorded during visual encounter surveys included age, sex, time, location, habitat, and notes of interest.

Road Surveys
Road surveys were conducted in the reptile and amphibian inventory. Although this technique was limited in its usefulness for the inventory, it did lead to the documentation of several important species of herpetofauna. Road surveys were conducted along Swegle Road and the historic site entrance in the evening and night hours during warm weather and lasted for several hours or until temperatures had cooled below the point at which reptile and amphibian activity could be expected.

Point Counts
The variable-circular plot point count was employed in 2002 to supplement visual encounters during the bird inventory and followed protocol outlined by Ralph et. al. (1995) and Reynolds et. al. (1980). While the point count is normally used to estimate species richness, abundance, and

density, the point count was used here as an inventory tool by enabling a single observer to systematically document common species across a relatively large area. Results from the point count also provided pilot data for monitoring.

Due to the small size of the historic site, only 6 point count stations were established (see Figure 2). A distance of approximately 250 meters was maintained between stations in order to avoid double counting of individual birds. Point counts were conducted between sunrise and 10 am between June 16-21, 2002. Birds flushed or observed during travel to stations were noted on the data sheet of the closest station. Point counts began 1 minute after arrival to the station to allow birds to resume normal activity. Counts lasted for 10 minutes and birds seen or heard and their distance from the station center were recorded in 10-meter increments. Ancillary information included time, location, weather, topography, and habitat.

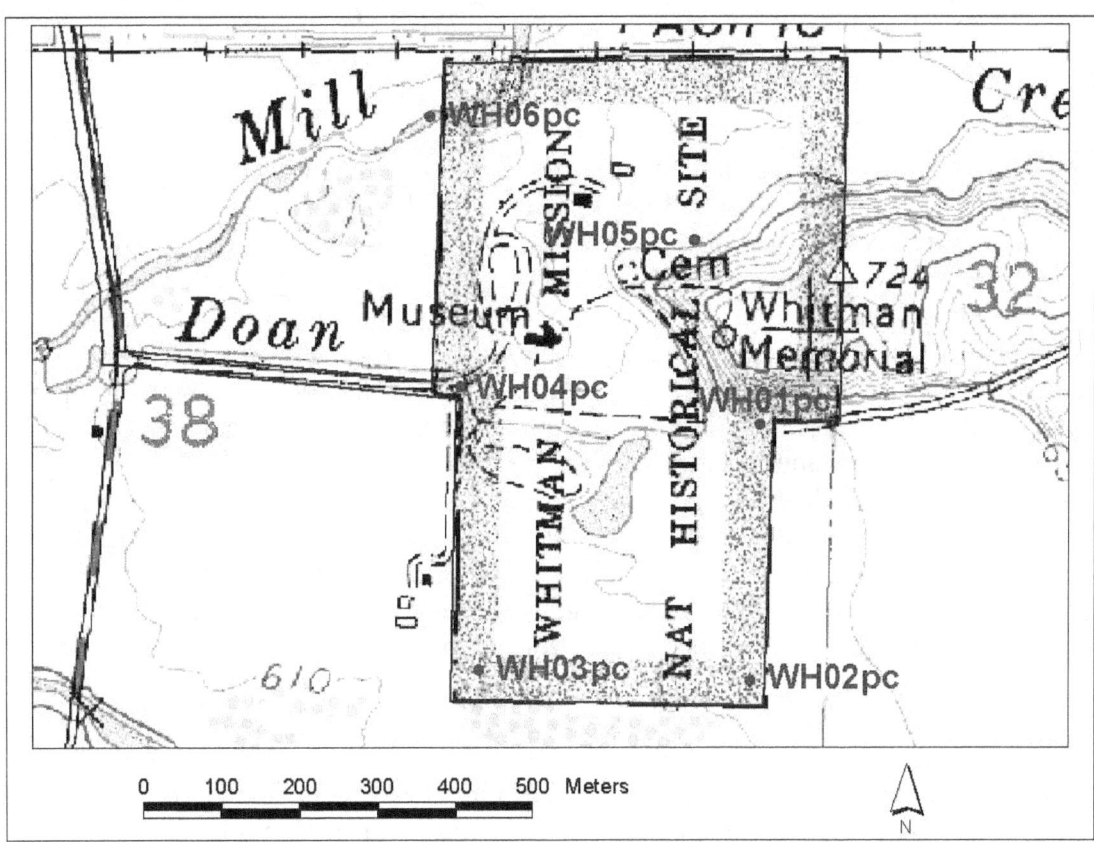

Figure 2. Location of point count stations established in June of 2002 at Whitman Mission National Historic Site.

Trapping

A variety of trapping techniques were used to inventory small mammals and bats and generally followed procedures outlined in Jones et al. (1996), Cooperrider et al. (1986), Kunz (1988), and the Upper Columbia Basin Network Study Plan (Wright et. al. unpublished). Capture and handling procedures were consistent with those outlined by the Ad Hoc Committee on Acceptable Field Methods in Mammalogy (1987) and the University of Idaho Institutional Animal Care and Use Committee.

Small Mammals

The primary technique used for small mammals involved the use of Sherman live traps and Museum Special snap traps placed along 50-meter transects. Trap stations were established approximately every 5 meters and 1 live trap and 1 snap trap was placed at each station. Some transects were pre-baited for 1 day and traps were set for two to four consecutive nights. Traps were placed non-randomly near microhabitat features and mammal sign in order to maximize capture success. Traps were baited with peanut butter, crimped oats, and black oil sunflower seeds. Liver and raw chicken was used to target shrews.

Miscellaneous trapping techniques included the use of Havahart wire cage traps targeted for skunks and weasels, and pitfalls employed for shrews, voles, and mice. Pitfall arrays consisted of 4 coffee cans set in the ground with 1.5-meter hardware cloth drift fence between each can. Small mammal trapping was conducted on June 16-21, 2002. Auxiliary data related with small mammal captures included time, date, location, weather, moon phase, topography, age, sex, and habitat.

Bats

Mist netting was the primary bat capture technique used in the inventory and generally followed methods outlined in Kunz (1988). Mist nets designed specifically for bats (i.e. 38mm mesh size with reduced bag) were placed over Mill Creek and the Walla Walla River under the Swegle Road bridges. This placement was chosen in an attempt to funnel bats into nets. Nets were also placed along the edge of the Mill Pond. A range of net lengths (2.6, 6, 9, and 12 meters) was used in different arrays in response to topographic and strategic considerations. Nets were opened at sunset and kept open until bat activity slowed down. Productive sites were revisited in order to detect seasonal and nightly variation in species presence. Ancillary data collected with bat captures included time of capture, date, location, weather, time of sunset, moon phase, age, sex, reproductive condition, forearm length, and habitat. Tissue samples were collected from little brown myotis (*Myotis lucifugus*) and Yuma myotis (*Myotis yumanensis*) for the purpose of confirming species identification using genetic techniques. These two species are very difficult to distinguish in the field and are often misidentified. A graduate student at Portland State University conducted the genetic analysis and confirmed species identifications (Scott, unpublished data).

Bat Acoustic Surveys

The Anabat bat detection system (Titley Electronics, Ballina, NSW, Ausralia; Corben Scientific, Rohnert Park, CA, USA) was used to supplement mist netting. Anabat allows for the recording and analysis of the ultrasonic calls emitted by bats during foraging and commuting. The Anabat system consisted of an Anabat II bat detector, type 6 standard Zero-Crossings Analysis Interface Module, an IBM-compatible laptop, Anabat 6 software, and Analook software. A 12-volt 100-watt handheld spotlight was used during recording sessions to illuminate flying bats and provide visual cues to aid in species identification. Species identification of free-flying bats was the primary application of Anabat in the inventory, although information on bat activity was also obtained from the use of Anabat. A library of Anabat call files was developed by recording calls emitted from bats released during capture sessions. The library was used to enhance the species identification of calls recorded from free-flying bats. Recordings of free-flying bats at Whitman Mission were compared with a larger call library developed during inventory work at the John Day Fossil Beds National Monument in central Oregon to aid in species identification

(Rodhouse, University of Idaho, unpublished data). The Anabat system was used simultaneously during mist netting sessions. Ancillary information collected with Anabat recording included time and location. Library calls included positive species identification, age, sex, forearm length, and notes of interest. Voucher calls were also obtained from individual little brown and Yuma myotis that had tissue samples taken from them. Results from the genetic analysis were used to analyze the calls from these two species and enhance the use of Anabat as a diagnostic tool for these two species in the field. A subset of voucher calls for each species confirmed in the historic site can be found in Appendix C of this report.

Species Documentation Methods

Species encountered during the inventory were documented using photography, voucher specimens from incidental mortality, and field observation records. Mammal specimens are permanently housed at the University of Washington Burke Museum of Natural History in Seattle, Washington. In addition to specimens and photographs, data sheets and field notes were kept on all inventory activities and species encountered. Photocopies have been made of all data sheets and field notes and are permanently housed with the Upper Columbia Basin Network. Voucher Anabat bat call recordings are included in Appendix C of this report.

Results

Historic Information

No comprehensive vertebrate inventory has been conducted in Whitman Mission prior to the current I & M project and little historic vertebrate information is available from the mission. Historic observations have been recorded in the 1962 historic site Master Plan and in a series of observation logs by past historic site staff (Jack Winchell, personal communication). The University of Idaho Cooperative Park Studies Unit conducted a study of the northern pocket gopher in the historic site in 1981 (Wright and Grabmiller 1981). A modest effort was made to document birds and mammals as part of a review of exotic plant pests in the mission in 1998 (Monello and Wright 1998).

Birds

Expected and Confirmed Species

A total of 117 birds were expected to occur in or near the mission and all of those species have been confirmed. As well, 85 unexpected species have also been confirmed, bringing the total number of birds confirmed in or near the mission to 202. These unexpected species are those that are migratory or vagrants and are not expected to regularly occur in the mission each year. Table 1 lists the expected and unexpected species and their confirmation status. Table 2 lists the results of point counts conducted in June of 2002.

Mammals

Expected and Confirmed Species

A total of 30 species of mammals are expected to occur in or adjacent to the mission. Twenty-seven species were documented during the inventory, including several species that were reported by historic site staff. Ninety percent of the mammals expected to occur in the historic site have been documented. The list of expected and possible species and their current status in the mission is shown in Table 3.

Small Mammals

Trapping effort for small and medium sized non-volant mammals totaled 575 trap nights. Total capture of non-volant mammals was 84 individuals. Deer mice (*Peromyscus maniculatus*) and montane voles were the most abundant mammals captured, representing 80% of all captures. The vagrant shrew (*Sorex vagrans*) was the third most abundant mammal captured, representing 17% of all captures. Table 4 shows the location and trapping effort information and Table 5 shows the results from the 2002 mammal trapping effort. Figure 3 shows the location of mammal traps in the historic site.

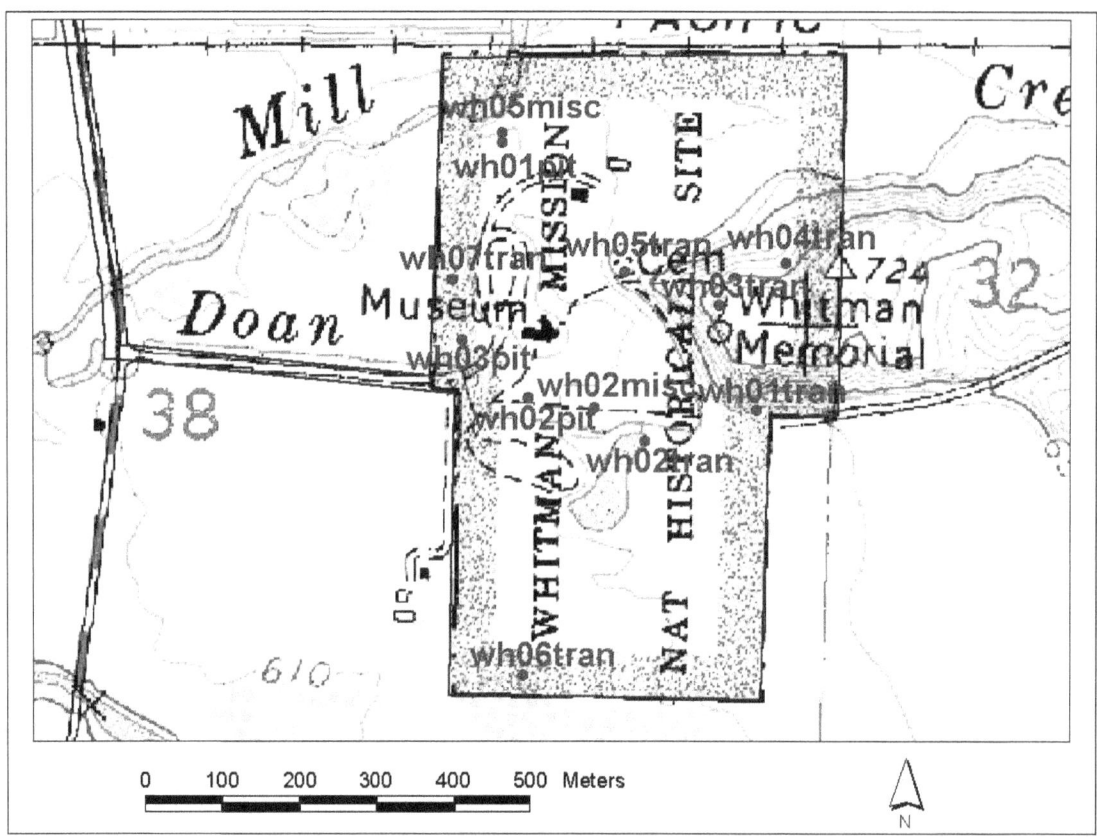

Figure 3. Location of mammal transects established during the 2002 inventory trapping sessions at Whitman Mission National Historic Site.

Bats

Mist netting for bats was conducted on 4 nights in 2002. Bat captures were lower than expected. Three species were captured; the Yuma myotis (*Myotis yumanensis*), the little brown myotis (*Myotis lucifugus*), and the silver-haired bat (*Lasionycteris noctivagans*). Table 6 shows the results from mist netting efforts in 2002.

The results of Anabat recording confirmed that the low mist net captures reflected low levels of activity during all 4 nights of investigation. The hoary bat (*Lasiurus cinereus*) and big brown bat (*Eptesicus fuscus*) were confirmed through the use of Anabat. Voucher recordings of bats at Whitman Mission are included in Appendix C of this document.

Amphibians and Reptiles

Expected and Confirmed Species

A total of 4 species of amphibians and 8 species of reptiles are expected to occur in and adjacent to Whitman Mission. The 2002-2003 inventory confirmed 8 of those species (67%), including the great basin spadefoot toad (*Spea intermontana*), a unique species of amphibian. Figure 4 shows the location of amphibians and reptiles encountered during the inventory. Table 7 shows the list of expected species and unexpected species and their status on the mission. Table 8 shows the location of herptetofauna encountered during the 2002-2003 inventory.

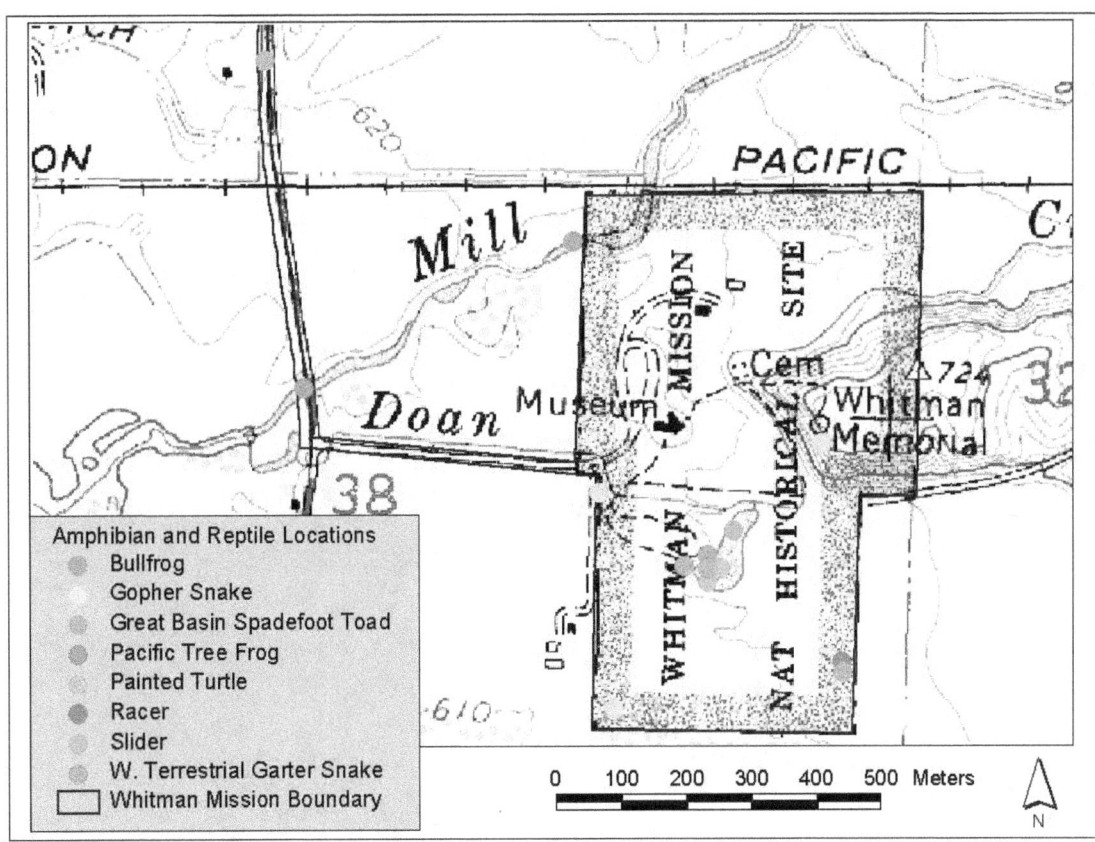

Figure 4. Location of amphibians and reptiles encountered during the 2002-2003 inventory at Whitman Mission National Historic Site.

Discussion

Birds

Whitman Mission supports a surprisingly rich diversity of bird life. A large proportion of the species are migratory and wintering birds, indicating the importance of the 98-acre parcel as a stop over for those species. The Mill Pond is used by many species of waterfowl and the riparian and grassland vegetation attract a wide variety of passerines. Of particular note are the many insectivorous flycatchers, vireos, and warblers that use the historic site as a migratory stop over and as a nesting area. Another important resource for birds is the dead and dying cottonwood trees found along Mill Creek and the Walla Walla River. These snags provide important resources for primary cavity nesters, such as the northern flicker (*Colaptes auratus*) and provides even more critical habitat to secondary cavity nesters such as the western screech owl (*Otus kennicottii*). Rookeries of black-crowned night herons (*Nycticorax nycticorax*) and great blue herons (*Ardea herodius*) exist along Mill Creek near the west boundary of the historic site.

Mammals

Whitman Mission supports several introduced species of mammals. The Virginia opossum (*Didelphis virginiana*), eastern cottontail (*Sylvilagus floridanus*), and eastern gray squirrel (*Sciurus carolinensis*) all occur in the mission. The eastern gray squirrel has only recently become established there. Historic site staff first reported seeing it in the historic site in 2002. We did not encounter it during visits to the historic site in 2002 but found it to be common in 2003. The house mouse (*Mus musculus*) is likely to occur in the historic site as well but has not yet been confirmed.

Bat activity in the historic site was much lower than expected in 2002. The area in and around the historic site provides good roosting and foraging habitat for many species of bats and we are unable to explain the lack of activity and diversity. The lack of nearby cliffs and extensive forests reduces the overall number of expected species, but males and nonbreeding females of many of those unexpected species could move through the Walla Walla Valley.

Amphibians and Reptiles

There are a number of other species of amphibians and reptiles that have been recorded nearby or in the general area of the Columbia Basin that are not considered likely to occur in the Whitman Mission Historical Site. Several inhabit rocky areas, and because there is no such significant habitat in the mission site, it is doubtful that they occur there. These are the western fence lizard (*Sceloporus occidentalis*), side-blotched lizard (*Uta stansburiana*), striped whipsnake (*Masticophis taeniatus*), night snake (*Hypsiglena torquata*), and western rattlesnake (*Crotalus viridis*). Local stories maintain that rattlesnakes inhabited the vicinity of the mission in past times, but were exterminated by farmers (Winchell personal communication).

The sagebrush lizard (*Sceloporus graciosus*) and pigmy short-horned lizard (*Phrynosoma douglasi*) require semi-arid shrubby environments with open, sandy soils. Although most of the mission site is densely carpeted with grass or shaded by trees, there is a small open remnant of mixed shrub-bunchgrass habitat on parts of the Memorial Hill. However, this is very limited and it is doubtful that these two reptiles are currently present there. Originally, Memorial Hill was primarily covered with sagebrush, but was heavily grazed by cattle before the historic site was established (Whitman Mission National Historic Site 2003). The Memorial Hill area grew back to rabbitbrush, along with many exotic grasses and other introduced plants. Recent restoration efforts have successfully reestablished native bunchgrasses there. There is one reported sighting by a visitor of "a lizard with blue sides", which may have been a sagebrush lizard. However, this cannot be confirmed.

Species that are more probable include several amphibians. Members of the grounds crew mentioned that salamanders with greenish-yellow markings are occasionally found under damp boards and leaf litter. These are probably the long-toed salamander (*Ambystoma macrodactylum*). There are three species of toads native to the region, the western toad (*Bufo boreas*), Woodhouse's toad (*Bufo woodhouseii*), and the Great Basin spadefoot toad (*Spea intermontana*). The spadefoot toad was documented in the mission in 2003. Although both species of *Bufo* toads may occur in the mission, both have experienced rangewide declines in recent decades and, after spending multiple summer nights searching for these species, are no longer expected (Corkran and Thoms 1996).

The northern leopard frog (*Rana pipiens*) inhabited the mission site in the past, with the last definite record being in 1962 (preserved in the Walla Walla College collection). Repeated searches were conducted in the mission area for leopard frogs from 1992 through 1996 but only non-native bullfrogs (*Rana catesbiana*) were found (Leonard et. al. 1999). These large, predatory amphibians eat almost any kind of smaller animal in their environment, and native frogs usually disappear when bullfrogs invade the same location. Some species of frogs are extremely sensitive to pesticides and herbicides. These toxins may have entered the aquatic systems of the mission site via runoff from lawns and flowerbeds and also contributed to the demise of the northern leopard frog.

The common garter snake (*Thamnophis sirtalis*) has also been found in the general area and probably occurs at the mission site. It differs from the western terrestrial garter snake in having brighter, more defined yellow stripes, along with a row of small red spots on a black background along the sides of the body. Former staff ranger Jack Winchell, described past sightings of two reptiles that have such unique morphological characteristics, that there is little doubt as to their identity. One is the rubber boa (*Charina bottae*) with its short, blunt, rounded-off tail and loose, rubbery skin. The other is the western skink (*Eumeces skiltonianus*). This small, secretive lizard is unmistakable with its electric-blue tail. These two species are also expected to occur in the historic site today.

Literature Cited

Ad hoc Committee on Acceptable Field Methods in Mammalogy. 1987. Acceptable field methods in mammalogy: preliminary guidelines approved by the American Society of Mammalogists. Journal of Mammalogy 68(4) supplement: 18 pp.

Burke Museum of Natural History and Culture. 2003. Burke Mammalogy Mammals of Washington. University of Washington Burke Museum of Natural History and Culture, Seattle, WA. http://www.Washington.edu/burkemuseum/mammalogy/mamwash/index.html. (accessed 12/18/2003).

Cooperrider, A.Y., R.J. Boyd, and H.R. Stuart. 1986. Inventory and monitoring of wildlife habitat. U.S. Dept. of Interior Bureau of Land Management Service Center. Denver, CO.

Corkran, C. C. and C.R. Thoms. 1996. Amphibians of Oregon, Washington, and British Columbia. Lone Pine Publishing, Renton, WA.

ITIS. 2003. Integrated taxonomic information system on-line database system. U.S. Department of Agriculture. http://www.itis.usda.gov. (accessed 1/10/03).

Jones, C., W.J. McSea, M.J. Conroy, and T.H. Kunz. 1996. Capturing mammals. *In* D.E. Wilson, F.R. Cole, J.D. Nichols, R. Rudran, and M.S. Foster (eds.) Measuring and monitoring biological diversity: standard methods for mammals. Smithsonian Institution Press, Washington D.C.

Leonard, W.P., K.R. McAllister, and R.C. Friesz. 1999. Survey and assessment of the northern leopard frog (*Rana pipiens*) populations in Washington state. Northwestern Naturalist 80:51-60.

Monello, R.J. and G.R. Wright. 1998. Exotic pest plan inventory, mapping, and priorities for control in parks in the Pacific Northwest, and initial bird and small mammal survey results for parks in the Pacific Northwest. USGS Idaho Cooperative Fish and Wildlife Research Unit, University of Idaho, Moscow, ID.

Peterson, R.T. 1990. A field guide to western birds. The Peterson Field Guide Series. Houghton Mifflin Co., Boston, MA.

Ralph, C.J., S. Droege, and J.R. Sauer. 1995. Managing and monitoring birds using point counts: standards and applications. USDA Forest Service Gen. Tech. Rep. PSW-GTR-149.

Reynolds, R.T., J.M. Scott, and R.A. Nussbaum. 1980. A variable circular-plot method for estimating bird numbers. Condor 82:309-313.

Sibley, D.A. 2000. The Sibley guide to the birds. National Audubon Society. Chanticleer Press, New York, NY.

St. John, A. D. 2002. Reptiles of the northwest: Alaska to California, rockies to the coast. Lone Pine Publishing, Renton, WA.

Verts, B.J. and L.N. Carraway. 1998. Land mammals of Oregon. University of California Press, Berkeley, CA.

Washington Department of Fish and Wildlife. 2003. Species of Concern. http://www.wdfw.wa.gov/wlm/diversity/soc/soc.htm. (accessed 12/18/2003).

Western Regional Climate Center. 2003. Idaho Climate Summaries. Desert Research Institute, Reno, NV. www.wrcc.dri.edu/summary/climsmid.html. (accessed 12/18/2003).

Whitman Mission National Historic Site. 2003. Nature and science overview. USDI National Park Service. http://www.nps.gov/whmi/pphtml/nature.html. (accessed 12/18/2003).

Wilson, D.E., F.R. Cole, J.D. Nichols, R. Rudran, and M.S. Foster. 1996. Measuring and monitoring biological diversity: Standard methods for mammals. Smithsonian Institution Press, Washington, D.C.

Wright, G.R., L. Garrett, and D. Foster. Unpublished. A study plan to inventory vascular plants and vertebrates in national park service units in the Upper Columbia Basin Network. University of Idaho Department of Fish and Wildlife. Moscow, ID.

Wright, G.R. and P. Grabmiller. 1981. Pocket gopher activity and potential control at Whitman Mission National Historic Site: Cooperative Park Studies Unit. Rep. B-81-6. University of Idaho, Moscow, ID.

Yensen, E. and P.W. Sherman. 2003. Ground dwelling squirrels of the Pacific Northwest. U.S. Fish and Wildlife Service, Snake River Fish and Wildlife Office, Boise, ID.

Appendix A. List of tables

Table 1. Confirmation status of expected and possible bird species located in or near Whitman Mission National Historic Site.

Common Name	Expected	Confirmed	Source[a]			
			A	B	C	D
Horned Grebe	0	0	0	0	0	0
Eared Grebe	0	1	0	0	0	1
Pied-billed Grebe	0	1	0	0	0	1
Double-crested Cormorant	0	1	0	1	0	1
American Bittern	0	1	0	0	0	1
Great Blue Heron	1	1	0	1	1	1
Great Egret	0	1	0	0	0	1
Snowy Egret	0	1	0	0	0	1
Cattle Egret	0	1	0	0	0	1
Black-crowned Night-Heron	1	1	0	1	0	1
White-faced Ibis	0	1	0	0	0	1
Turkey Vulture	1	1	0	0	0	1
Greater White-fronted Goose	0	1	0	0	0	1
Snow Goose	0	1	0	0	0	1
Ross's Goose	0	1	0	0	0	1
Canada Goose	1	1	0	1	1	1
Brant	0	1	0	0	0	1
Tundra Swan	0	1	0	0	0	1
Wood Duck	1	1	1	1	0	1
Gadwall	1	1	0	0	0	1
Eurasian Wigeon	0	1	0	0	0	1
American Wigeon	1	1	0	0	0	1
Mallard	1	1	0	1	1	1
Blue-Winged Teal	1	1	0	0	0	1
Cinnamon Teal	1	1	0	0	0	1
Northern Shoveler	1	1	0	0	0	1
Northern Pintail	1	1	0	0	0	1
Green-winged Teal	1	1	0	0	0	1
Redhead	1	1	0	0	0	1
Canvasback	1	1	0	0	0	1
Greater Scaup	0	1	0	0	0	1
Lesser Scaup	1	1	0	0	0	1
Bufflehead	1	1	0	0	0	1
Common Goldeneye	1	1	0	0	0	1
Barrow's Goldeneye	0	1	0	0	0	1
Hooded Merganser	0	1	0	0	0	1
Common Merganser	0	1	0	0	0	1
Ruddy Duck	1	1	0	0	0	1
Osprey	1	1	0	0	1	1
Bald Eagle	1	1	0	0	0	1
Northern Harrier	1	1	1	1	1	1
Sharp-shinned Hawk	1	1	1	0	0	1
Cooper's Hawk	1	1	0	0	0	1

Table 1. Confirmation status of expected and possible bird species located in or near Whitman Mission National Historic Site (continued).

Common Name	Expected	Confirmed	Source[a]			
			A	B	C	D
Northern Goshawk	0	1	0	0	0	1
Swainson's Hawk	1	1	1	1	1	1
Red-tailed Hawk	1	1	0	1	1	1
Ferruginous Hawk	0	1	0	0	0	1
Rough-legged Hawk	1	1	0	0	0	1
Golden Eagle	0	1	0	0	0	1
American Kestrel	1	1	1	1	1	1
Merlin	0	1	0	0	0	1
Prairie Falcon	0	1	0	0	0	1
Peregrine Falcon	0	1	0	0	0	1
Gray Partridge	1	1	0	0	0	1
Ring-necked Pheasant	1	1	0	1	1	1
Wild Turkey	1	1	0	0	0	1
California Quail	1	1	0	1	1	1
Northern Bobwhite	1	1	0	0	0	1
Virginia Rail	1	1	0	0	0	1
Sora	0	1	0	0	0	1
American Coot	1	1	0	0	0	1
Sandhill Crane	1	1	0	0	0	1
Semipalmated Plover	0	1	0	0	0	1
Killdeer	1	1	0	0	1	1
Black-necked Stilt	0	1	0	0	0	1
American Avocet	0	1	0	0	0	1
Greater Yellowlegs	0	1	0	0	0	1
Lesser Yellowlegs	0	1	0	0	0	1
Solitary Sandpiper	0	1	0	0	0	1
Spotted Sandpiper	1	1	0	1	1	1
Long-billed Curlew	0	1	0	0	0	1
Least Sandpiper	0	0	0	0	0	0
Western Sandpiper	0	1	0	0	0	1
Baird's Sandpiper	0	1	0	0	0	1
Pectoral Sandpiper	0	1	0	0	0	1
Short-billed Dowitcher	0	1	0	0	0	1
Long-billed Dowitcher	0	1	0	0	0	1
Common Snipe	0	1	0	0	0	1
Wilson's Phalarope	1	1	0	0	0	1
Red Phalarope	0	1	0	0	0	1
Red-necked Phalarope	0	1	0	0	0	1
Bonaparte's Gull	0	1	0	0	0	1
Ring-billed Gull	1	1	1	1	1	1
California Gull	1	1	0	1	0	1
Herring Gull	0	1	0	0	0	1
Glaucous-winged Gull	1	1	0	0	0	1
Glaucous Gull	0	1	0	0	0	1
Caspian Tern	0	1	0	0	0	1

Table 1. Confirmation status of expected and possible bird species located in or near Whitman Mission National Historic Site (continued).

Common Name	Expected	Confirmed	Source[a]			
			A	B	C	D
Common Tern	0	1	0	0	0	1
Black Tern	0	1	0	0	0	1
Rock Dove	1	1	0	0	0	1
Mourning Dove	1	1	1	1	1	1
Barn Owl	1	1	0	1	0	1
Western Screech Owl	1	1	0	1	0	1
Great Horned Owl	1	1	0	1	0	1
Snowy Owl	0	1	0	0	0	1
Long-eared Owl	0	1	0	0	0	1
Short-eared Owl	1	1	0	0	0	1
Northern Saw-whet Owl	0	1	0	0	0	1
Common Nighthawk	1	1	0	0	0	1
Common Poorwill	0	1	0	0	0	1
Vaux's Swift	1	1	0	1	1	1
Black-chinned Hummingbird	1	0	0	0	0	0
Calliope Hummingbird	0	1	0	0	0	1
Rufous Hummingbird	1	1	0	0	0	1
Belted Kingfisher	1	1	0	1	1	1
Lewis's Woodpecker	0	1	0	0	0	1
Williamson's Sapsucker	0	1	0	0	0	1
Red-naped Sapsucker	0	1	0	0	0	1
Downy Woodpecker	1	1	1	1	0	1
Hairy Woodpecker	1	1	0	0	0	1
Northern Flicker	1	1	1	1	1	1
Pileated Woodpecker	0	1	0	0	0	1
Olive-sided Flycatcher	0	1	0	0	0	1
Western Wood-Pewee	1	1	1	1	1	1
Willow Flycatcher	0	1	0	0	0	1
Hammond's Flycatcher	0	1	0	0	0	1
Cordilleran Flycatcher	1	1	0	0	1	1
Dusky Flycatcher	1	1	0	0	1	1
Western Kingbird	1	1	0	1	1	1
Eastern Kingbird	1	1	0	0	0	1
Loggerhead Shrike	1	1	0	0	0	1
Northern Shrike	1	1	0	0	0	1
Warbling Vireo	1	1	0	0	0	1
Cassin's Vireo	0	1	0	0	0	1
Red-eyed Vireo	0	1	0	0	0	1
Steller's Jay	0	1	0	0	0	1
Black-billed Magpie	1	1	1	1	1	1
American Crow	1	1	1	1	1	1
Common Raven	1	1	0	0	0	1
Horned Lark	0	1	0	0	0	1
Tree Swallow	1	1	0	0	0	1
Violet-green Swallow	1	1	0	0	1	1

Table 1. Confirmation status of expected and possible bird species located in or near Whitman Mission National Historic Site (continued).

Common Name	Expected	Confirmed	Source[a]			
			A	B	C	D
Northern Rough-winged Swallow	1	1	1	1	1	1
Bank Swallow	1	1	0	1	1	1
Cliff Swallow	1	1	0	1	1	1
Barn Swallow	1	1	1	1	1	1
Black-capped Chickadee	1	1	0	1	1	1
Mountain Chickadee	1	1	0	0	0	1
Bushtit	0	0	0	0	0	0
White-breasted Nuthatch	0	0	0	0	0	0
Red-breasted Nuthatch	1	1	0	1	0	1
Brown Creeper	1	1	0	0	0	1
Rock Wren	0	1	0	0	0	1
Bewick's Wren	1	1	1	1	1	1
House Wren	1	1	1	1	1	1
Winter Wren	1	1	0	0	0	1
Marsh Wren	0	1	0	0	0	1
Golden-crowned Kinglet	0	0	0	0	0	0
Ruby-crowned Kinglet	1	1	0	0	1	1
Western Bluebird	1	1	0	0	0	1
Mountain Bluebird	1	1	0	0	0	1
Townsend's Solitaire	1	1	0	0	0	1
Veery	0	1	0	0	0	1
Swainson's Thrush	0	1	0	0	0	1
Hermit Thrush	0	1	0	0	0	1
American Robin	1	1	1	1	1	1
Varied Thrush	0	1	0	0	0	1
Gray Catbird	0	1	0	0	0	1
European Starling	1	1	1	1	1	1
American Pipit	0	1	0	0	0	1
Bohemian Waxwing	0	1	0	0	0	1
Cedar Waxwing	1	1	0	0	0	1
Orange-crowned Warbler	1	1	0	0	0	1
Nashville Warbler	0	1	0	0	0	1
Yellow Warbler	1	1	0	1	1	1
Yellow-rumped Warbler	1	1	0	0	0	1
Townsend's Warbler	1	1	0	0	0	1
MacGillivray's Warbler	0	1	0	0	0	1
Common Yellowthroat	0	1	0	0	0	1
Wilson's Warbler	1	1	0	0	1	1
Yellow-breasted Chat	0	1	0	0	0	1
Western Tanager	1	1	0	0	0	1
Spotted Towhee	1	1	0	0	1	1
American Tree Sparrow	0	1	0	0	0	1
Chipping Sparrow	1	1	0	0	0	1
Brewer's Sparrow	0	1	0	0	0	1
Vesper Sparrow	1	1	0	0	0	1

Table 1. Confirmation status of expected and possible bird species located in or near Whitman Mission National Historic Site (continued).

Common Name	Expected	Confirmed	Source[a]			
			A	B	C	D
Lark Sparrow	1	1	0	0	0	1
Savannah Sparrow	1	1	0	0	0	1
Grasshopper Sparrow	0	1	0	0	0	1
Fox Sparrow	1	1	0	0	0	1
Song Sparrow	1	1	1	1	1	1
Lincoln's Sparrow	1	1	0	0	0	1
White-throated Sparrow	0	1	0	0	0	1
Harris's Sparrow	0	1	0	0	0	1
White-crowned Sparrow	1	1	0	0	1	1
Golden-crowned Sparrow	1	1	0	0	0	1
Dark-eyed Junco	1	1	0	0	0	1
Lapland Longspur	0	1	0	0	0	1
Black-headed Grosbeak	1	1	1	1	1	1
Lazuli Bunting	1	1	0	0	0	1
Red-winged Blackbird	1	1	1	1	1	1
Western Meadowlark	1	1	0	1	1	1
Yellow-headed Blackbird	0	1	0	0	0	1
Brewer's Blackbird	1	1	0	1	1	1
Brown-headed Cowbird	1	1	1	1	1	1
Bullock's Oriole	1	1	0	1	1	1
Gray-crowned Rosy Finch	0	1	0	0	0	1
Cassin's Finch	1	1	0	0	0	1
House Finch	1	1	1	0	1	1
Red Crossbill	0	1	0	0	0	1
White-winged Crossbill	0	1	0	0	0	1
Common Redpoll	0	1	0	0	0	1
Pine Siskin	1	1	0	0	0	1
Lesser Goldfinch	0	0	0	0	0	0
American Goldfinch	1	1	1	1	1	1
Evening Grosbeak	1	1	0	0	1	1
House Sparrow	1	1	0	1	1	1
Total Confirmed	**117**	**202**				
Total % Confirmed		**1.00[b]**				

[a] A = University of Idaho 2001 fieldwork (Rita Dixon); B = University of Idaho 2002 fieldwork (Tom Rodhouse); C = University of Idaho 2003 fieldwork (Tom Rodhouse); D = Sightings recorded by Mike Denny, Blue Mountain Audubon Society, Walla Walla.
[b] Percentage based on 117 confirmed expected species and does not include 85 additional confirmed unexpected species.

Table 2. Results from bird point counts conducted at Whitman Mission National Historic Site in June 2002. (Species are listed in order of discovery rather than in taxonomic order)

Common Name	Count Station[a]						Total
	A	B	C	D	E	F	
Black-billed Magpie	5	4	4		3	1	17
Red-winged Blackbird	6		1	5	5	1	18
Ring-necked Pheasant	1	1	1	1		1	5
Black-headed Grosbeak	3	1					4
Song Sparrow	1	2	1	1	2	1	8
California Quail	1	4					5
Bank Swallow	4	18	20	1	2	1	46
Brewer's Blackbird	2						2
Bewick's Wren	1	2	1		2		6
American Robin	1			5	1		7
Ringbilled Gull	2				1		3
House Wren		2	2	1		1	6
Western Wood Pewee		1			1		2
Northern Flicker		1			1		2
Yellow Warbler		1				1	2
Downy Woodpecker		1		1			2
Swainson's Hawk		1	1				2
Mourning Dove		2	2				4
European Starling			3			1	4
Barn Swallow			1				1
Brown-headed Cowbird			1	1	1		3
American Goldfinch				2	1	1	4
Black-capped Chickadee					1		1
Belted Kingfisher					1		1
American Crow					2	4	6
Red-tailed Hawk						3	3
California Gull						1	1
Black-crowned Night Heron						3	3
Spotted Sandpiper						1	1
Northern Rough-winged Swallow						1	1
Total	**27**	**41**	**38**	**18**	**24**	**22**	**170**

[a] A=WH01pc, B=WH02pc, C=WH03pc, D=WH04pc, E=WH05pc, F=WH06pc

Table 3. Confirmation status of expected and possible mammal species located at Whitman Mission National Historic Site

Common Name	Expected	Confirmed
Virginia Opossum	1	1
Vagrant Shrew	1	1
Coast Mole	1	0
California Myotis	0	0
Long-eared Myotis	0	0
Little Brown Myotis	1	1
Fringed Myotis	0	0
Long-legged Myotis	0	0
Yuma Myotis	1	1
Hoary Bat	1	1
Silver-haired Bat	1	1
Big Brown Bat	1	1
Townsend's Big-eared Bat	0	0
Pallid Bat	0	0
Eastern Cottontail	1	1
Mountain Cottontail	1	0
Black-tailed Jackrabbit	0	0
Yelow-bellied Marmot	0	0
Columbian Ground Squirrel	1	1
Eastern Gray Squirrel	1	1
Northern Pocket Gopher	1	1
Great Basin Pocket Mouse	1	1
American Beaver	1	1
Western Harvest Mouse	1	1
Deer Mouse	1	1
Northern Grasshopper Mouse	0	0
Bushy-tailed Woodrat	0	0
House Mouse	1	0
Long-tailed Vole	0	0
Montane Vole	1	1
Common Muskrat	1	1
Western Jumping Mouse	0	0
Common Porcupine	1	1
Coyote	1	1
Red Fox	0	0
Common Raccoon	1	1
Long-tailed Weasel	1	1
Mink	1	1
American Badger	1	1
River Otter	0	0
Western Striped Skunk	1	1
Western Spotted Skunk	0	0
Mountain Lion	0	0
Bobcat	1	1
Elk	0	0

Table 3. Confirmation status of expected and possible mammal species located at Whitman Mission National Historic Site (continued).

Common Name	Expected	Confirmed
White-tailed Deer	1	1
Mule Deer	1	1
Total	**30**	**27**
Total % Confirmed		**0.90**

Table 4. Location, trap type, and number of trap nights for mammal trap transects, miscellaneous trap locations, Havahart trap locations, pitfall locations, and mist net locations in Whitman Mission during the 2002-2003 inventory.

Capture Session	Date	Location	UTM X	UTM Y	Trap Nights	Trap Type
wh01tran	6/19/02	East Boundary	387102	5099359	60	Sherman/Snap
wh02tran	6/19/02	East Boundary	386959	5099320	60	Sherman/Snap
wh03tran	6/19/02	Memorial Hill	387055	5099490	60	Sherman/Snap
wh04tran	6/19/02	Memorial Hill	387139	5099543	60	Sherman/Snap
wh05tran	6/17/02	Irrigation Canal	386933	5099531	40	Sherman/Snap
wh06tran	6/19/02	South Boundary	386801	5099027	60	Sherman/Snap
wh07tran	6/19/02	West Boundary	386710	5099522	60	Sherman/Snap
wh01misc	6/17/02	Irrigation Canal	386933	5099531	10	Snap
wh02misc	6/17/02	Irrigation Canal	386895	5099361	100	Sherman/Snap
wh03misc	6/17/02	Variable	x	x	10	Havahart
wh04misc	6/19/02	Oregon Trail Area	x	x	15	Havahart
wh05misc	6/19/02	Mill Creek	386775	5099705	10	Snap
wh01pit	6/17/02	Mill Creek	386775	5099693	12	Pitfalls
wh02pit	6/18/02	Oregon Trail Area	386809	5099374	9	Pitfalls
wh03pit	6/18/02	Entrance	386722	5099446	9	Pitfalls
wh01mist	6/19/02	Walla Walla Bridge	386222	5099031		Mist Net
wh02mist	6/20/02	Mill Creek Bridge	386268	5099553		Mist Net
wh04mist	8/12/02	Mill Creek Bridge	386268	5099553		Mist Net
wh03mist	8/11/02	Mill Pond	386811	5099505		Mist Net
Total					**575**	

Table 5. Capture results from small mammal trapping efforts during the 2002-2003 inventory in Whitman Mission.

Capture Session	SOVA	PEPA	REMA	PEMA	MIMO	Total
wh01tran					7	7
wh02tran	4			4	6	14
wh03tran		1		7	2	10
wh04tran		1		7	1	9
wh05tran				2		2
wh06tran			2	13		15
wh07tran				1	1	2
wh01misc						0
wh02misc	6				12	18
wh03misc						0
wh04misc						0
wh05misc						0
wh01pit	1				2	3
wh02pit	3					3
wh03pit					1	1
Total	**14**	**2**	**2**	**34**	**32**	**84**
Relative Abundance	**0.17**	**0.02**	**0.02**	**0.40**	**0.38**	

Table 6. Capture results from mist net sessions during the 2002-2003 inventory in Whitman Mission.

Capture Session	MYYU	MYLU	LANO	Total
wh01mist		1		1
wh02mist		1	4	5
wh03mist				0
wh04mist	2	2		4
Total	**2**	**4**	**4**	**10**
Relative Abundance	**0.2**	**0.4**	**0.4**	

Table 7. Confirmation status of expected or possible amphibian and reptile species at Whitman Mission National Historic Site.

Amphibians	Expected	Confirmed
Northern Long Toed Salamander	1	0
Tiger Salamander	0	0
Pacific Tree Frog	1	1
Great Basin Spadefoot Toad	1	1
Western Toad	0	0
Woodhouse's Toad	0	0
Bullfrog	1	1
Total Amphibians	**4**	**3**
Total % Confirmed		**0.75**

Reptiles	Expected	Confirmed
Painted Turtle	1	1
Slider	1	1
Western Skink	1	0
Rubber Boa	1	0
Racer	1	1
Gopher Snake	1	1
Western Terrestrial Garter Snake	1	1
Common Garter Snake	1	0
Total Reptiles	**8**	**5**
Total % Confirmed		**0.63**

Table 8. Location of amphibian and reptile encounters during the 2002-2003 inventory at Whitman Mission National Historic Site.

Date	Species	UTM X	UTM Y
6/18/02	Pacific Tree Frog	386183	5099783
6/19/02	Pacific Tree Frog	386594	5099961
8/9/03	Great Basin Spadefoot Toad	386210	5100001
6/18/02	Bullfrog	386882	5099242
8/9/03	Bullfrog	386882	5099242
6/18/02	Painted Turtle	386882	5099242
8/9/03	Painted Turtle	386882	5099242
6/18/02	Slider	386882	5099242
8/9/03	Slider	386882	5099242
8/9/03	Racer	387090	5099093
6/19/02	Gopher Snake	386740	5099033
6/20/02	Gopher Snake	386718	5099355
6/21/02	Gopher Snake	387058	5099429
6/19/02	Western Terrestrial Garter Snake	386882	5099242
6/19/02	Western Terrestrial Garter Snake	386882	5099242
6/19/02	Western Terrestrial Garter Snake	386848	5099246
6/19/02	Western Terrestrial Garter Snake	386848	5099246
6/19/02	Western Terrestrial Garter Snake	386922	5099298
6/20/02	Western Terrestrial Garter Snake	387091	5099088
6/20/02	Western Terrestrial Garter Snake	387091	5099088
6/20/02	Western Terrestrial Garter Snake	387091	5099088
6/21/02	Western Terrestrial Garter Snake	387091	5099088
6/21/02	Western Terrestrial Garter Snake	387091	5099088
8/9/03	Western Terrestrial Garter Snake	386922	5099298

Appendix B. Species Account

This section gives a brief description of each expected or unexpected but possible species for the Whitman Mission National Historic Site. Species names are followed by a series of codes based on those in use by the National Park Service NPSpecies database. The first code indicates site confirmation status, followed by species abundance and species residency. The information presented here is based on the 2002-2003 inventory results, bird sighting information contributed by Mike Denny, Blue Mountain Audubon Society, and Whitman Mission staff. It is important to note that abundance is based on relative estimates founded on inventory results rather than quantitative population estimates. A key to the codes used after the species names is below.

Historic Site Status

- **(P) Present:**
  Species occurrence in park is documented and assumed to be extant.
- **(H) Historic:**
  Species historical occurrence in the park is documented, but recent investigations indicate that the species is now probably absent.
- **(PP) Probably Present:**
  Park is within species range and contains appropriate habitat. Documented occurrences of the species in the adjoining region of the park give reason to suspect that it probably occurs within the park. The degree of probability may vary within this category, including species that range from common to rare.
- **(E) Encroaching**
  The species is not documented in the park, but is documented as being adjacent to the park and has potential to occur in the park.
- **(U) Unconfirmed:**
  Included for the park based on weak (unconfirmed) record or no evidence, giving minimal indication of the species occurrence in the park.
- **(FR) False Report:**
  Species previously reported to occur within the park, but current evidence indicates that the report was based on a misidentification, a taxonomic concept no longer accepted, or some other similar problem of interpretation.

Species Abundance

- **Abundant:**
  May be seen daily, in suitable habitat and season, and counted in relatively large numbers.
  (C) Common:
  May be seen daily, in suitable habitat and season, but not in large numbers.
  (U) Uncommon:
  Likely to be seen monthly in appropriate season/habitat. May be locally common.
  (R) Rare:
  Present, but usually seen only a few times each year.
  (O) Occasional:
  Occurs in the park at least once every few years, but not necessarily every year. Applicable to animals only.
- **(UNK) Unknown:**
  Abundance unknown.

Residency

- **(B) Breeder:**
  Population reproduces in the park.
- **(R) Resident:**
  A significant population is maintained in the park for more than two months each year, but it is not known to breed there.
- **(M) Migratory:**
  Migratory species that occurs in park approximately two months or less each year and does not breed there.
- **(V) Vagrant:**
  Park is outside of the species usual range.
- **(UNK) Unknown:**
  Residency status in park is unknown.

Birds

Species	Status	Abundance	Breeding
Horned Grebe *Podiceps auritus*	Unexpected		
Eared Grebe *Podiceps nigricollis*	Present	U	M
Pied-billed Grebe *Podilymbus podiceps*	Present	U	M
Double-crested Cormorant *Phalacrocorax auritus*	Present	U	M
American Bittern *Botaurus lentiginosus*	Present	R	UNK
Great Blue Heron *Ardea herodias*	Present	C	B
Great Egret *Ardea alba*	Present	U	M
Snowy Egret *Egretta thula*	Present	R	M
Cattle Egret *Bulbulcus ibis*	Present	R	M
Black-crowned Night Heron *Nycticorax nycticorax*	Present	C	B
White-faced Ibis *Plegadis chihi*	Present	O	M
Turkey Vulture *Cathartes aura*	Present	U	UNK
Greater White-fronted Goose *Anser albifrons*	Present	R	M
Snow Goose *Chen caerulescens*	Present	R	M
Ross's Goose *Chen rossii*	Present	O	V
Canada Goose *Branta canadensis*	Present	C	B
Brant *Branta bernicula*	Present	O	V
Tundra Swan *Cygnus columbianus*	Present	R	M
Wood Duck *Aix sponsa*	Present	C	B
Gadwall *Anas strepera*	Present	U	R
Eurasian Wigeon *Anas penelope*	Present	O	M
American Widgeon *Anas Americana*	Present	U	R

Mallard *Anas platyrhynchos*	Present	C	B
Blue-winged Teal *Anas discors*	Present	R	UNK
Cinnamon Teal *Anas cyanoptera*	Present	R	UNK
Northern Shoveler *Anas clypeata*	Present	U	UNK
Northern Pintail *Anas acuta*	Present	R	R
Green-winged Teal *Anas crecca*	Present	U	UNK
Canvasback *Aythya valisineria*	Present	R	UNK
Redhead *Aythya Americana*	Present	R	UNK
Greater Scaup *Aythya marila*	Present	U	M
Lesser Scaup *Aythya affinis*	Present	C	R
Bufflehead *Bucephala albeola*	Present	U	R
Common Goldeneye *Bucephala clangula*	Present	U	R
Barrow's Goldeneye *Bucephala islandica*	Present	R	M
Hooded Merganser *Lophodytes cucullatus*	Present	R	R
Common Merganser *Mergus merganser*	Present	R	R
Ruddy Duck *Oxyura jamaicensis*	Present	U	R
Osprey *Pandion haliaetus*	Present	U	R
Bald Eagle *Haliaetus albicilla*	Present	U	R

This species is a threatened species under the federal endangered species act (Washington Department of Fish and Wildlife 2003).

Northern Harrier *Circus cyaneus*	Present	C	B
Sharp-shinned Hawk *Accipiter striatus*	Present	U	R
Cooper's Hawk *Accipiter cooperii*	Present	R	R
Northern Goshawk *Accipiter gentilis*	Present	R	M

This species is a federal species of concern and probably occurs in the historic site sporadically in winter (Washington Department of Fish and Wildlife 2003).

Swainson's Hawk *Buteo swainsoni*	Present	C	B
Red-tailed Hawk *Buteo jamaicensis*	Present	C	B
Ferruginous Hawk *Buteo regalis*	Present	R	UNK

This species is a federal species of concern and probably occurs only sporadically in the Walla Walla Valley (Washington Department of Fish and Wildlife 2003).

Rough-legged Hawk *Buteo lagopus*	Present	R	R
Golden Eagle *Aquila chrysaetos*	Present	R	UNK
American Kestrel *Falco sparverius*	Present	C	B
Merlin *Falco columbarius*	Present	R	R
Prairie Falcon *Falco mexicanus*	Present	U	UNK
Peregrine Falcon *Falco peregrinus*	Present	R	M

This species was recently removed from the federal endangered species act but remains a federal species of concern (Washington Department of Fish and Wildlife 2003).

Gray Partridge *Perdix perdix*	Present	R	B
Ring-necked Pheasant *Phasianus colchicus*	Present	C	B
Wild Turkey *Melleagris gallopavo*	Present	U	B
California Quail *Callipepla californica*	Present	C	B
Northern Bobwhite *Colinus virginianus*	Present	U	B
Virginia Rail *Rallus limicola*	Present	U	UNK
Sora *Porzana carolina*	Present	R	UNK
American Coot *Fulica americana*	Present	U	R
Sandhill Crane *Grus canadensis*	Present	U	M

This species is a state endangered species but rarely occurs in the mission during migration (Washington Department of Fish and Wildlife 2003).

Species			
Semipalmated Plover *Charadrius semipalmatus*	Present	O	M
Killdeer *Charadrius vociferous*	Present	U	B
Black-necked Stilt *Himantopus mexicanus*	Present	O	M
American Avocet *Recurvirostra americana*	Present	O	M
Greater Yellowlegs *Tringa melanoleuca*	Present	O	M
Lesser Yellowlegs *Tringa flavipes*	Present	O	M
Solitary Sandpiper *Tringa solitaria*	Present	O	M
Spotted Sandpiper *Actitis macularia*	Present	U	M
Long-billed Curlew *Numenius americanus*	Present	R	UNK
Least Sandpiper *Calidris minutilla*	Unexpected		
Western Sandpiper *Calidris mauri*	Present	R	M
Baird's Sandpiper *Calidris bairdii*	Present	O	M
Pectoral Sandpiper *Calidris melanotos*	Present	O	M
Short-billed Dowitcher *Limnodromus griseus*	Present	O	M
Long-billed Dowitcher *Limnodromus scolopaceae*	Present	O	M
Common Snipe *Gallinago gallinago*	Present	R	B
Wilson's Phalarope *Phalaropus tricolor*	Present	R	UNK
Red Phalarope *Phalaropus fulicaria*	Present	O	M
Red-necked Phalarope *Phalaropus lobatus*	Present	O	M
Bonaparte's Gull *Larus philedelphia*	Present	O	M
Ring-billed Gull *Larus delawarensis*	Present	C	UNK
California Gull *Larus californicus*	Present	C	UNK

Herring Gull *Larus argentatus*	Present	R	R	
Glaucous-winged Gull *Larus glaucescens*	Present	R	R	
Glaucous Gull *Larus hyperboreus*	Present	O	M	
Caspian Tern *Sterna caspia*	Present	R	M	
Common Tern *Sterna hirundo*	Present	O	M	
Black Tern *Sterna forsteri*	Present	O	M	

This species is a federal species of concern and occurs sporadically in the mission during migration (Washington Department of Fish and Wildlife 2003).

Rock Dove *Columba livia*	Present	U	B	
Mourning Dove *Zenaida macroura*	Present	C	B	
Barn Owl *Tyto alba*	Present	U	B	
Western Screech Owl *Otus kennicottii*	Present	U	B	
Great-horned Owl *Bubo virginianus*	Present	U	B	
Snowy Owl *Nyctea scandinaca*	Present	O	V	
Long-eared Owl *Asio otus*	Present	R	UNK	
Short-eared Owl *Asio flammeus*	Present	R	UNK	
Northern Saw-whet Owl *Aegolius acadicus*	Present	O	M	
Common Nighthawk *Chordeiles minor*	Present	U	B	
Common Poorwill *Phalaenoptilus nuttallii*	Present	UNK	UNK	
Vaux's Swift *Chaetura vauxi*	Present	U	B	
Black-chinned Hummingbird *Archilochus alexandri*	Present	R	UNK	
Calliope Hummingbird *Stellula calliope*	Present	R	M	
Rufous Hummingbird *Selasphorous rufus*	Present	R	M	

Belted Kingfisher *Ceryle alcyon*	Present	U	B
Lewis's Woodpecker *Melanerpes lewis*	Present	R	M
Williamson's Sapsucker *Sphyrapicus varius*	Present	R	M
Red-naped Sapsucker *Sphyrapicus nuchalis*	Present	R	M
Downy Woodpecker *Picoides pubescens*	Present	U	B
Hairy Woodpecker *Picoides villosus*	Present	R	R
Northern Flicker *Colaptes auratus*	Present	C	B
Pileated Woodpecker *Dryocopus pileatus*	Present	R	UNK
Western Wood Pewee *Contopus sordidulus*	Present	C	B
Willow Flycatcher *Empidonax traillii*	Present	R	UNK

This species is a federal species of concern and its status in the mission is uncertain (Washington Department of Fish and Wildlife 2003).

Hammond's Flycatcher *Empidonax hammondii*	Present	O	M
Cordilleran Flycatcher *Empidonax occidentalis*	Present	R	M
Dusky Flycatcher *Empidonax oberholseri*	Present	R	M
Western Kingbird *Tyrannus verticalis*	Present	C	B
Eastern Kingbird *Tyrannus tyrannus*	Present	R	B
Loggerhead Shrike *Lanius ludovicianus*	Present	R	UNK

This species is a federal species of concern and its status in the mission is uncertain (Washington Department of Fish and Wildlife 2003).

Northern Shrike *Lanius excubitor*	Present	R	R
Warbling Vireo *Vireo gilvus*	Present	U	UNK
Cassin's Vireo *Vireo cassinii*	Present	R	M
Red-eyed Vireo *Vireo olivaceus*	Present	R	M

Steller's Jay *Cyanocitta stelleri*	Present	O	M
Black-billed Magpie *Pica pica*	Present	A	B
American Crow *Corvus brachyrhyncos*	Present	C	B
Common Raven *Corvus corax*	Present	R	UNK
Horned Lark *Eremophila alpestris*	Present	U	R
Tree Swallow *Tachycineta bicolor*	Present	R	B
Violet-green Swallow *Tachycineta thalassina*	Present	U	B
Northern Rough-winged Swallow *Stelgidopteryx serripennis*	Present	C	B
Bank Swallow *Riparia riparia*	Present	C	B
Cliff Swallow *Petrochelidon pyrrhonata*	Present	C	B
Barn Swallow *Hirundo rustica*	Present	C	B
Black-capped Chickadee *Poecile atricapillus*	Present	U	R
Mountain Chickadee *Poecile gambeli*	Present	U	R
Bushtit *Psaltriparus flaviceps*	Unexpected		
White-breasted Nuthatch *Sitta carolinensis*	Unexpected		
Red-breasted Nuthatch *Sitta canadensis*	Present	U	UNK
Brown Creeper *Certhia americana*	Present	R	UNK
Rock Wren *Salpinctes obsoletus*	Present	R	UNK
Bewick's Wren *Thryomanes bewickii*	Present	A	B
House Wren *Troglodytes aedon*	Present	C	B
Winter Wren *Troglodytes troglodytes*	Present	R	R
Marsh Wren *Cistothorus palustris*	Present	R	R
Golden-crowned Kinglet *Regulus satrapa*	Unexpected		

Ruby-crowned Kinglet *Regulus calendula*	Present	U	UNK
Western Bluebird *Sialia mexicana*	Present	R	UNK
Mountain Bluebird *Sialia currucoides*	Present	R	R
Townsend's Solitaire *Myadestes townsendi*	Present	R	R
Veery *Catharus fuscescens*	Present	R	M
Swainson's Thrush *Catharus ustulatus*	Present	R	M
Hermit Thrush *Catharus guttatus*	Present	R	M
American Robin *Turdus migratorius*	Present	A	B
Varied Thrush *ixoreus navius*	Present	R	M
Gray Catbird *Dumetella carolinensis*	Present	R	UNK
European Starling *Sturnus vulgaris*	Present	A	B
American Pipit *Anthus rubescens*	Present	R	M
Bohemian Waxwing *Bombycilla garrulus*	Present	R	M
Cedar Waxwing *Bombycilla cedrorum*	Present	U	R
Orange-crowned Warbler *Vermivora celata*	Present	U	M
Nashville Warbler *Vermivora ruficapilla*	Present	R	M
Yellow Warbler *Dendroica petechia*	Present	C	B
Yellow-rumped Warbler *Dendroica coronata*	Present	U	R
Townsend's Warbler *Dendroica townsendi*	Present	R	R
Macgillivray's Warbler *Oporornis tolmiei*	Present	R	M
Common Yellowthroat *Geothlypis trichas*	Present	R	UNK
Wilson's Warbler *Wilsonia pusilla*	Present	U	M
Yellow-breasted Chat *Icteria virens*	Present	R	UNK

Western Tanager *Piranga ludoviciana*	Present	R	M
Spotted Towhee *Pipilo maculates*	Present	U	B
American Tree Sparrow *Spizella arborea*	Present	R	R
Chipping Sparrow *Spizella passerina*	Present	R	UNK
Brewer's Sparrow *Spizella breweri*	Present	R	UNK
Vesper Sparrow *Poocetes gramineus*	Present	R	UNK

The Oregon subspecies, *P.gramineus affinis* is listed as a federal species of concern but the subspecies that occurs in the mission is not known at this time (Washington Department of Fish and Wildlife 2003).

Lark Sparrow *Chondestes grammacus*	Present	R	UNK
Savannah Sparrow *Passerculus sandwichensis*	Present	R	M
Grasshopper Sparrow *Ammodramus savannarum*	Present	UNK	UNK
Fox Sparrow *Passerella iliaca*	Present	R	R
Song Sparrow *Melospiza melodia*	Present	C	B
Lincoln's Sparrow *Melospiza lincolnii*	Present	U	M
White-throated Sparrow *Zonotrichia albicollis*	Present	O	M
Harris's Sparrow *Zonotrichia querula*	Present	O	V
White-crowned Sparrow *Zonotrichia leucophrys*	Present	C	R
Golden-crowned Sparrow *Zonotrichia atricapilla*	Present	U	R
Dark-eyed Junco *Junco hyemalis*	Present	C	R
Lapland Longspur *Calcarius lapponicus*	Present	O	V
Black-headed Grosbeak *Pheuticus melanocephalus*	Present	C	B
Lazuli Bunting *Passerina amoena*	Present	U	B
Red-winged Blackbird *Agelaius phoeniceus*	Present	C	B

Western Meadowlark *Sturnella neglecta*   Present   U   B

Yellow-headed Blackbird *Xanthocephalus xanthocephalus*   Present   R   UNK

Brewer's Blackbird *Euphagus cyanocephalus*   Present   C   B

Brown-headed Cowbird *Molothrus ater*   Present   C   B

Bullock's Oriole *Icterus bullockii*   Present   C   B

Gray-crowned Rosy Finch *Leucosticte tephrocotis*   Present   O   V

Cassin's Finch *Carpodacus cassinii*   Present   U   R

House Finch *Carpodacus mexicanus*   Present   C   B

Red Crossbill *Loxia curvirostra*   Present   R   M

White-winged Crossbill *Loxia leucoptera*   Present   O   V

Common Redpoll *Carduelis flammea*   Present   O   V

Pine Siskin *Carduelis pinus*   Present   U   R

Lesser Goldfinch *Carduelis psaltria*   Unexpected

American Goldfinch *Carduelis tristis*   Present   C   B

Evening Grosbeak *Coccothraustes vespertinus*   Present   C   UNK

House Sparrow *Passer domesticus*   Present   C   B

Mammals

Vagrant Shrew *Sorex vagrans*　　　　　Present　　　C　　B

This species is common in the historic site, especially in moist areas with dense grasses and shrubs. Doan Creek and Mill Pond are particularly good locations for this species.

Coast Mole *Scapanus orarius*　　　　　Probably Present

This species probably occurs in the mission but need to be confirmed through trapping techniques specifically targeting this species.

California Myotis *Myotis californicus*　　　Unexpected

Long-eared Myotis *Myotis evotis*　　　　Unexpected

Little Brown Myotis *Myotis lucifugus*　　　Unexpected

Fringed Myotis *Myotis thysanodes*　　　　Unexpected

Long-legged Myotis *Myotis volans*　　　　Unexpected

Yuma Myotis *Myotis yumanensis*　　　　Present　　　C　　B

This species was captured along Mill Creek and the Walla Walla River and was recorded at the Mill Pond. This species is currently ranked as a federal species of concern (Washington Department of Fish and Wildlife 2003).

Hoary Bat *Lasiurus cinereus*　　　　　Present　　　U　　M

This species was seen, heard, and recorded flying along the cottonwood trees east of the Mill Pond in August 2002. This migratory species probably occurs sporadically in the historic site.

Silver-haired Bat *Lasionycteris noctivagans*　　　Present　　　U　　M

This species was captured in June of 2002. Like the hoary bat, this migratory species probably occurs sporadically in the historic site.

Big Brown Bat *Eptesicus fuscus*　　　　Present　　　C　　B

This species was seen and recorded along Mill Creek and at the Mill Pond.

Townsend's Big-eared Bat *Corynorhinus townsendii*　　　Unexpected

This federal species of concern is probably quite rare in the Walla Walla Valley. While it may occur in the vicinity of the historic site, it is not expected.

Pallid Bat *Antrozous pallidus*   Unexpected

This species is rare in southeastern Washington and is not expected in the historic site.

Eastern Cottontail *Sylvilagus nuttallii*   Present   C   B

This species is common throughout the historic site

Mountain Cottontail *Sylvilagus nuttallii*   Probably Present

The mountain cottontail probably occurs along with the eastern cottontail but could not be confirmed.

Black-tailed Jackrabbit *Lepus califoricus*   Unexpected

This species probably occurred in the historic site area historically, but was extirpated following extensive conversion of the Walla Walla Valley to agriculture.

Yellow-bellied Marmot *Marmota flaviventris*   Unexpected

This species probably occurs in isolated rocky localities in the Walla Walla Valley but is not expected to occur in the historic site.

Columbian Ground Squirrel *Spermophilus columbianus* Present   C   B

This species is found along the east boundary of the historic site along the base of the memorial hill and also occurs near the staff housing and maintenance buildings north of the visitor center.

Eastern Gray Squirrel *Sciurus carolinensis*   Present   C   B

The eastern gray squirrel has recently become established in the historic site. It apparently spread west from the city of Walla Walla, where it has been established for many years.

Northern Pocket Gopher *Thomomys talpoides*   Present   C   B

The mounds and tunnels formed by the species were observed throughout the historic site during the inventory. Several subspecies of *T. talpoides* are listed as candidate species by the state of Washington and the subspecies of the northern pocket gopher occurring in the mission has not yet been confirmed (Washington Department of Fish and Wildlife 2003).

Great Basin Pocket Mouse *Perognathus parvus* Present   C   B

The great basin pocket mouse was captured in the restored bunchgrass habitat on top of the memorial hill. This species is probably restricted to that area in the historic site. The presence of this species in the historic site may be a direct benefit from the restoration activities conducted in the historic site in recent years.

Beaver *Castor canadensis*   Unexpected

This species probably occurs in the Walla Walla Valley but is not expected to occur near the historic site.

Western Harvest Mouse *Reithrodontomys microps*   Present   U   B

This species was captured in the weedy grass habitat south of the Mill Pond.

House Mouse *Mus musculus*   Probably Present

This exotic species probably occurs in the historic site but has not yet been confirmed.

Deer Mouse *Peromyscus maniculatus*   Present   A   B

This ubiquitous species is abundant and was captured throughout the historic site.

Bushy-tailed Woodrat *Neotoma cinerea*   Unexpected

This species probably occurs in the Walla Walla Valley in rocky areas but is not expected to occur in the historic site.

Montane Vole *Microtus montanus*   Present   A   B

The montane vole was abundant in the moist grass habitats throughout the historic site.

Long-tailed Vole *Microtus longicaudus*   Unexpected

This species probably occurs in the Walla Walla Valley where more extensive stands of shrub grasslands occur.

Muskrat *Ondatra zibethicus*   Present   U   B

This species occurs along Mill Creek and the Walla Walla River and periodically is seen in the Mill Pond.

Western Jumping Mouse *Zapus princeps*   Unexpected

This species is probably restricted to the Blue Mountains south and east of the Walla Walla Valley and does not occur near the historic site.

Porcupine *Erethizon dorsatum*   Present   U   B

Historic site staff occasionally sees this species in the mission.

Coyote *Canis latrans*   Present   R   UNK

The coyote is periodically observed in the historic site.

Red Fox *Vulpes vulpes*   Unexpected

This species may occur in the Walla Walla Valley but is much more rare now with the extensive agriculture in the area.

Common Raccoon *Procyon lotor*   Present   U   B

This species occurs throughout the mission.

Long-tailed Weasel *Mustela erminea*   Present   U   B

This species has been periodically spotted by historic site staff, including one sighting of a female and young along the Oregon Trail near the Mill Pond.

Mink *Mustela vison*   Probably Present

American Badger *Taxidea taxus*   Present   R   UNK

This species occurs in and adjacent to the historic site.

River Otter *Lutra canadensis*   Unexpected

This species probably occurs in the Walla Walla River but is not expected to occur in the historic site.

Spotted Skunk *Spilogale gracilis*   Unexpected

This species is secretive and difficult to detect. This species likely occurs in the Walla Walla Valley but is not expected to occur in the historic site.

Striped Skunk *Mephitis mephitis*   Present   U   B

The striped skunk occurs throughout the Walla Walla Valley, including the historic site.

Mountain Lion *Puma concolor*   Unexpected

This wide-ranging species may occur in the Walla Walla Valley occasionally but is not expected to occur in the historic site.

Bobcat *Lynx rufus*   Present   R   UNK

This species has been seen on several occasions in recent years by historic site staff.

Elk *Cervus elaphus*   Unexpected

This species occurs in more remote portions of the Walla Walla Valley but is not likely to occur near the historic site.

White-tailed Deer *Odocoileus virginianus* Present   C   B

This species occurs throughout the mission.

Mule Deer *Odocoileus hemionus*   Present   C   B

This species occurs throughout the mission.

Amphibians

Northern Long-toed Salamander *Ambystoma macrodactylum*   Probably Present

This species probably occurs in the mission. Historic site staff reported seeing a salamander that fits this description in the past.

Tiger Salamander *Ambystoma tigrinum*   Unexpected

Great Basin Spadefoot Toad *Spea intermontana*   Present   R   B

This species was encountered crossing Swegle Road north of the Mill Creek Bridge in August, 2003.

Western Toad *Bufo boreas*   Unexpected

Woodhouse's Toad *Bufo woodhousii*   Unexpected

Pacific Treefrog *Hyla regilla*   Present   C   B

Several of these tiny frogs were heard calling in the area at night. All were just outside the mission site along Mill Creek. Two were heard under the bridge that crosses this stream on Swegle Road, and a small chorus was detected along this watercourse near the northwestern boundary. Despite repeated visits at night to the millpond, none were ever heard there (possibly due to predation by Bullfrogs).

Bullfrog *Rana catesbeiana*   Present   C   B

These large frogs are native to the regions east of the Rocky Mountains and have been introduced into the area of the mission. They are thriving and a large population was found inhabiting the millpond, Mill Creek, and Doan Creek.

Northern Leopard Frog *Rana pipiens*   Historic

This species was documented in the mission in the early 1960's. Subsequent searches for the species were unsuccessful and it has been determined that the species was extirpated from the Mission and probably most of the lower Walla Walla River valley (Leonard et. al 1999).

Reptiles

Painted Turtle *Chrysemys picta*   Present   C   B

These colorful reptiles were frequently found basking in the sun on a wooden raft that floats in the millpond. Many others were observed floating on the surface of the water. Four subspecies are recognized across this turtle's coast-to-coast range. One, the Western Painted Turtle (*C. p. bellii*) occurs in the Pacific Northwest.

Slider *Trachemys scripta*   Present   U   B

At least three of these introduced turtles were observed sunning on the floating wooden raft in the millpond. It is probable that this constitutes a small breeding population. The Slider is naturally native to portions of North America east of the Rocky Mountains.

Western Skink *Eumeces skiltonianus*   Probably Present

Mission site staff have reported historic sightings of snakes fitting the description of this species.

Rubber Boa *Charina bottae*   Probably Present

Mission site staff have reported historic sightings of snakes fitting the description of this species.

Racer *Coluber constrictor*   Present   U   B

This species was encountered in the brush pile in the southeast corner of the historic site in August 2003. This brushpile was also the location of several other reptile encounters and probably provides important cover for several species of reptiles and other vertebrates.

Gopher Snake *Pituophis catenifer*   Present   C   B

Three of these constrictors were found during the inventory in 2002. All three of the snakes from the mission site showed characteristics of the two subspecies native to the Washington-Oregon region: the Pacific Gopher Snake (*P. c. catenifer*), and the Great Basin Gopher Snake (*P. c. deserticola*). Apparently, this portion of the Columbia Basin is in an area of intergradation for these two geographical variations.

Western Terrestrial Garter Snake *Thamnophis elegans*   Present   C   B

This was the most frequently encountered snake in the mission site. Despite its misleading common name, this species is usually aquatic in its choice of habitats east of the Cascade Mountains. Most of the twelve individuals found during the inventory were never far from the millpond, an irrigation canal, Doan Creek, Mill Creek, or the Walla Walla River. Four of these reptiles were observed in one of the few places in the entire area where there is a large log with other smaller logs and branches piled next to it. This jumble of wood seems to provide much-needed cover for the snakes. It is located in the far southeastern corner of the mission site at the edge of a small grassy opening among low cottonwoods. Six subspecies are currently recognized, with the Wandering Garter Snake (*T. e. vagrans*) being the race inhabiting the Columbia Basin.

Appendix C. Voucher call recordings of bats confirmed at Whitman Mission National Historic Site

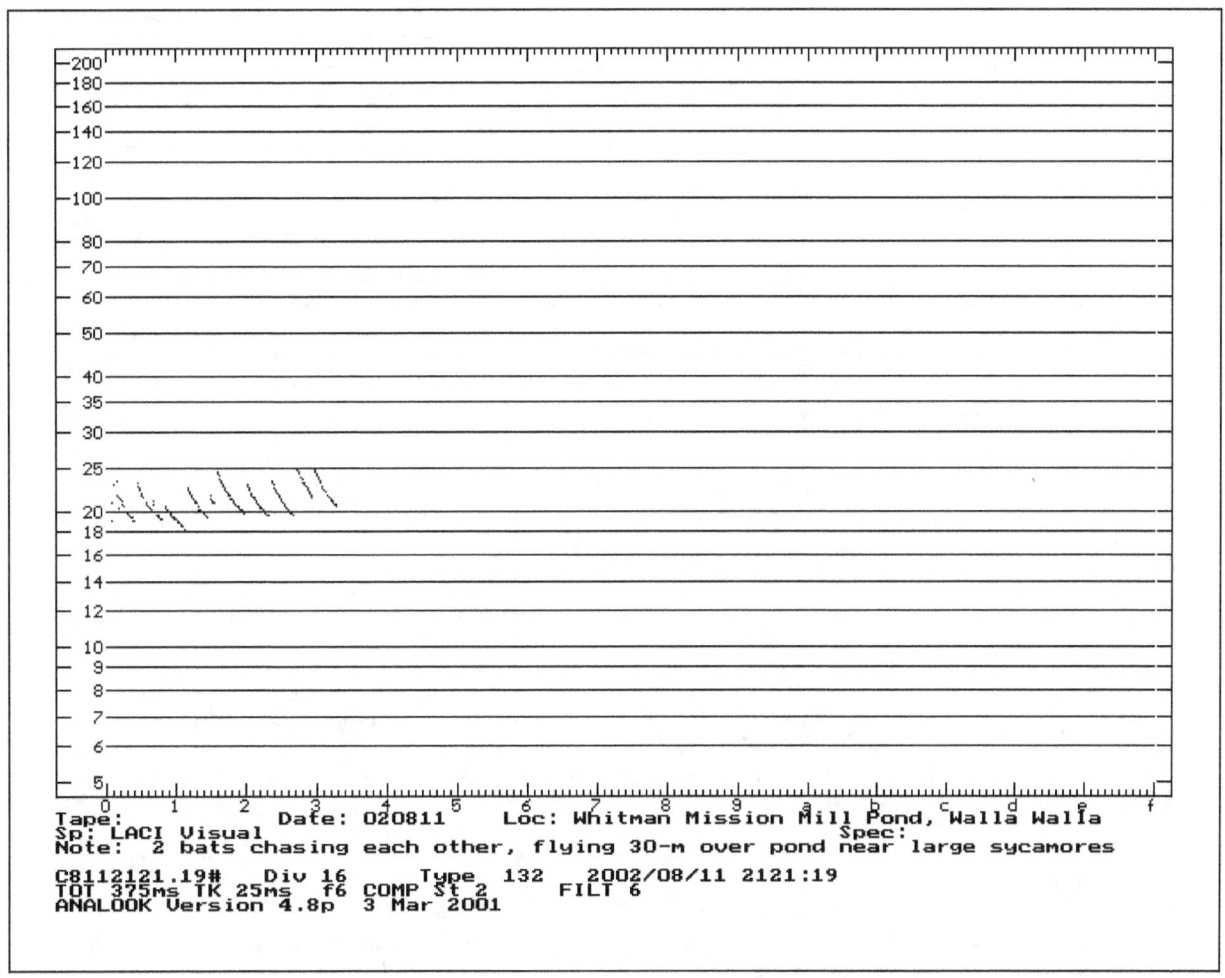

Figure C-1. Recording of a hoary bat (*Lasiurus cinereus*) flying along the edge of the Mill Pond. Two hoary bats were heard and spotlighted chasing each other during this recording but only 1 bat was picked up in the bat detector.

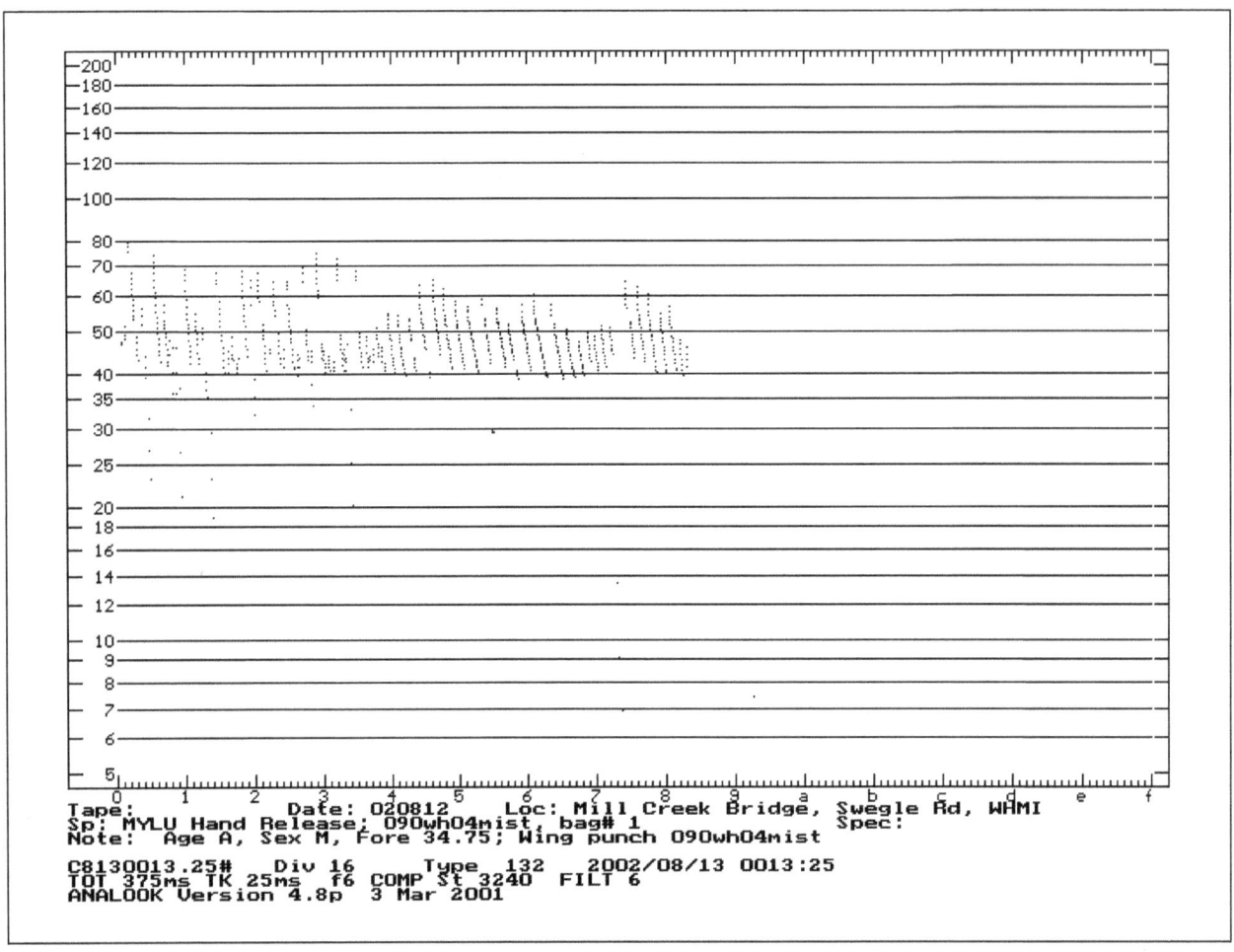

Figure C-2. Recording of a hand released little brown myotis (*Myotis lucifugus*) captured at the Mill Creek Bridge. This species identification of this individual was subsequently confirmed through genetic analysis from a tissue sample collected during the capture session.

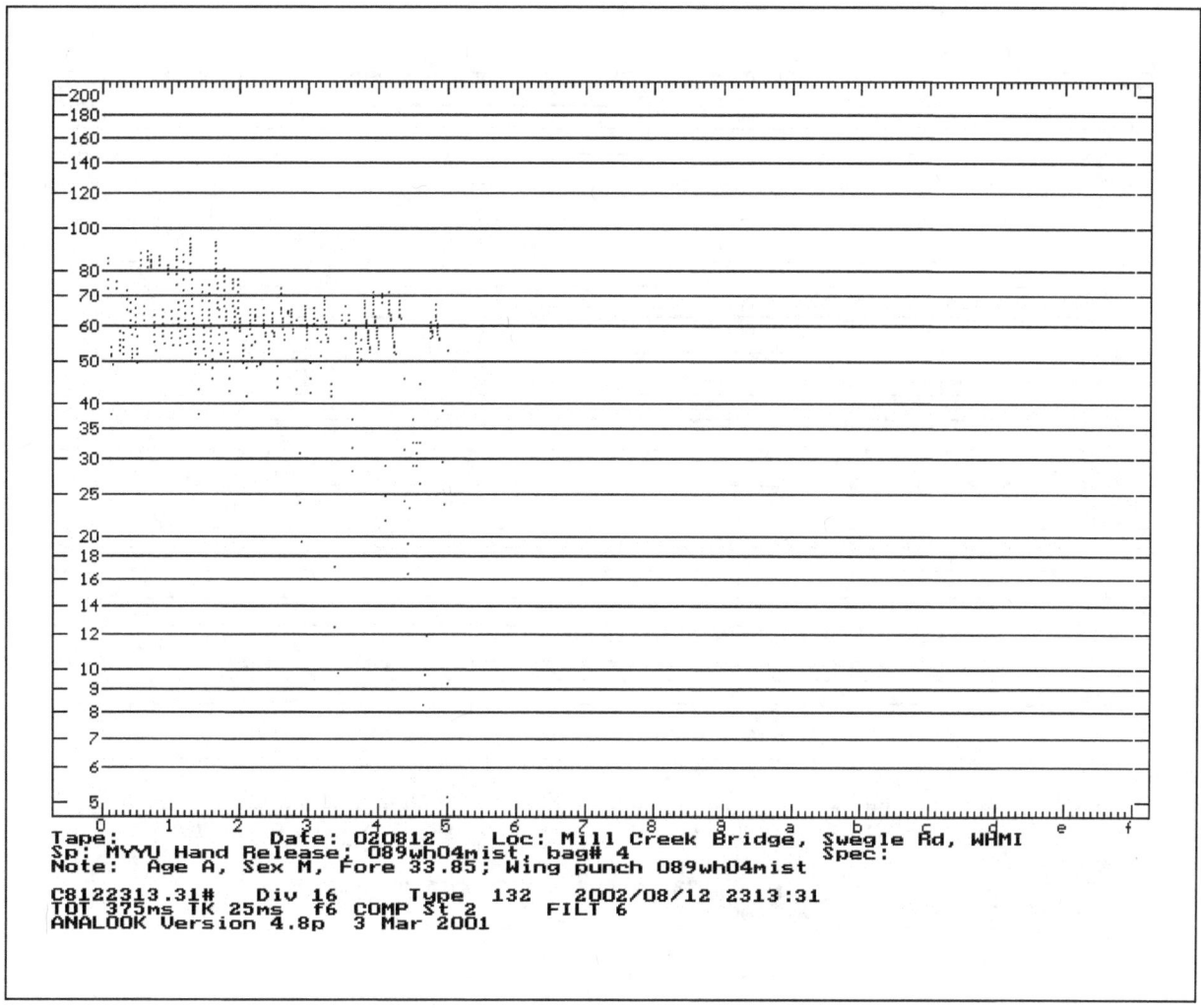

Figure C-3. Recording of a hand released Yuma myotis (*Myotis yumanensis*) captured at the Mill Creek Bridge. The species identification of this individual was confirmed through genetic analysis of a tissue sample collected during the capture session.

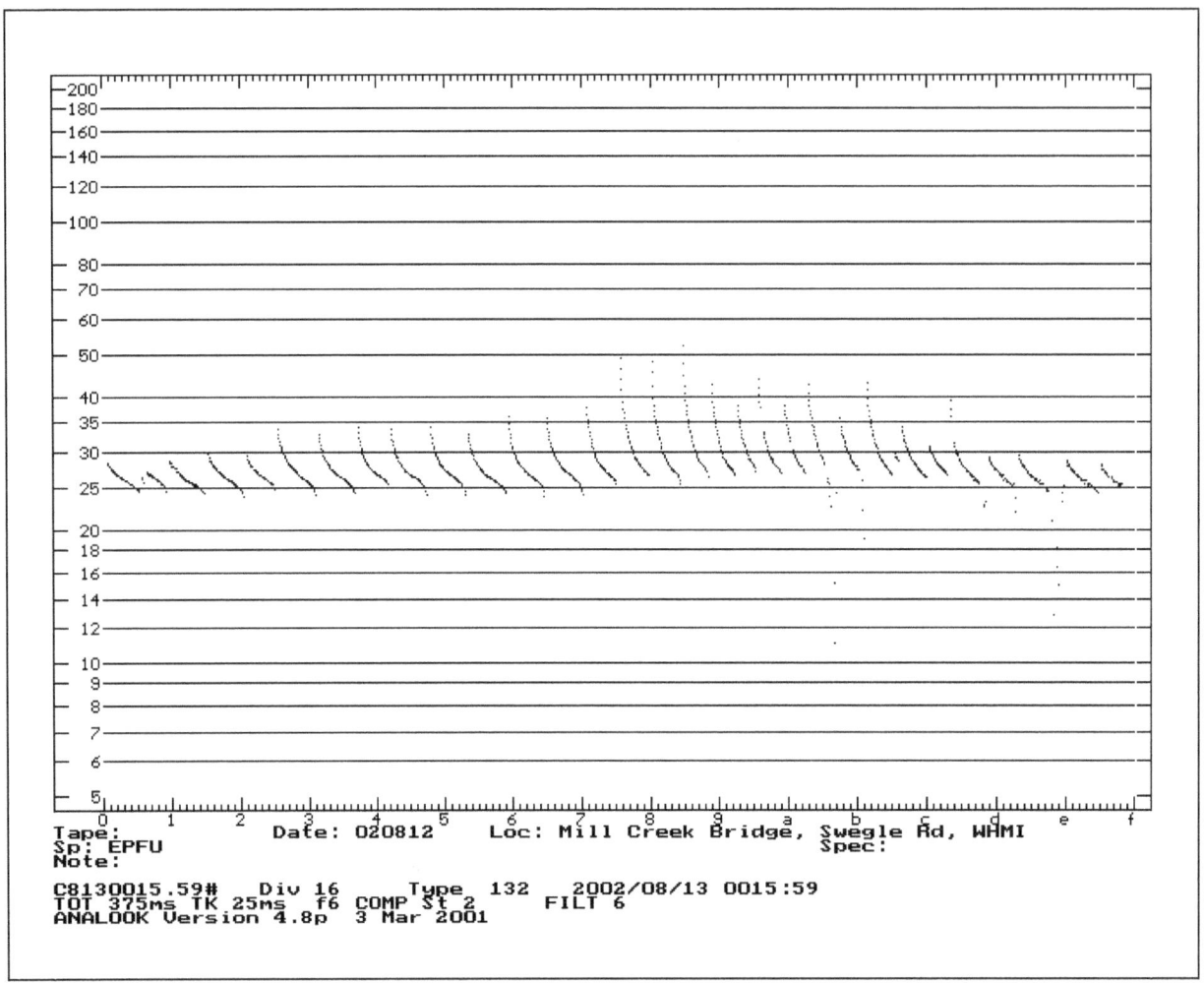

Figure C-4. Recording of a big brown bat (*Eptesicus fuscus*) observed flying overhead at the Mill Creek Bridge.

NPS 371/100878, January 2010

www.ingramcontent.com/pod-product-compliance
Lightning Source LLC
Chambersburg PA
CBHW081144290526
45795CB00006B/2372